HOW ALLENDE F

HOW ALLENDE FELL

A STUDY IN U.S.–CHILEAN RELATIONS

James F. Petras
and
Morris H. Morley

SPOKESMAN BOOKS 1974

Published by the Bertrand Russell Peace Foundation Ltd
Bertrand Russell House
Gamble Street, Nottingham
for *Spokesman Books*

Printed in Great Britain
by Bristol Typesetting Co Ltd
Barton Manor, Bristol

Contents

Introduction

A number of publications have appeared which discuss the relationship between U.S. policy towards the Allende government and its subsequent overthrow by a military junta in September 1973. A substantial number of these accounts have tended to dismiss or minimise the impact of U.S. policies on Chile's internal political situation during this three-year period, and to argue that the country's internal economic problems were essentially a product of the Allende government's incompetence and ineptness. This position has been repeatedly advanced by U.S. policy makers, and echoed in semi-official publications of the government as well as in academic circles. A sampling of this genre of argumentation is summarised in the following paragraphs :

'. . . the fault lies principally with an effort to redistribute income, an effort to bring about the fundamental structural changes to which the chairman referred in his opening statement . . . the basic reasons for the deterioration of the economy lie in the policies of the Government.'[1]

'. . . the economic policies themselves that were pursued by the Allende government resulted in the steadily deteriorating economic situation. The unwillingness of the government to modify its policies made it inevitable that international lending agencies would curtail their programmes for Chile . . . The Paris Club, consisting of various creditor nations, concluded there was little that could be done for Chile unless the government adopted policies they could support. I repeat, however, that it was not the United States, but the institutions themselves, which made their decisions. In sum it is untrue to say that the U.S. Government was responsible—either directly or indirectly —for the overthrow of Allende.'[2]

'. . . it was the policies of the Allende government, its insistence on forcing the pace beyond what the traffic would bear much more than our policies that contributed to their economic chaos.'[3]

'The argument that an American invisible blockade was responsible for or a major contributing factor to the overthrow of Allende is . . . not persuasive . . . the economic and political policies of the Allende government were a failure, in and of themselves.'[4]

'It seems quite likely, however, that by the latter part of 1972, the credit squeeze was a drop in the bucket as far as the causes of Chile's economic difficulties were concerned. The real causes were the internal matters . . . If any group can be said to be responsible, however, it was the extreme left which ultimately did bring down the Allende government . . . they never gave a chance to the constitutional road to socialism . . . In sum : the total credit picture of Chile may not have been anything like as bad as is sometimes made out : certainly not by the latter part of 1972. The real problem was lagging exports due to copper production losses; and soaring imports of food because of the failure of agriculture and Dr. Allende's desire to *more* than compensate for this—despite the lack of means.'[5]

Essentially these accounts in effect, by commission and omission, absolve the U.S. government and private enterprise of having had any significant impact on the course of events in Chile. By arguing that it was the Allende Government which created the conditions for the military coup, the implication is that the coup was 'inevitable' and (among some writers) justified. In more general terms the arguments imply that efforts to redistribute income and promote rapid and effective changes such as those envisaged by the democratic socialist government are doomed to failure because of their intrinsic impracticality.

It is not our purpose here to consider the above-mentioned accounts' totally inadequate discussion of the economic and political behaviour of the internal opposition (political formations, social classes and military officials) and their impact on the economy. What we are interested in documenting is the fact that Chile was heavily in debt *prior* to Allende's coming to power; that most of these debts were contracted with public, private and

8

international banks subject to U.S. influence; that payments on these unproductive debts incurred by earlier régimes came due during the Allende period; that the U.S. demand for debt payments became one instrument of U.S. economic pressure, that the cut-off of credits and loans was part of an overall U.S. policy to undermine the Allende Government; that U.S. policy was neither haphazard nor improvised but followed directly from the highest policy-making circles which incorporated the *political-economic interests of the U.S. in the region as a whole* as their primary consideration; that U.S. officials *chose* to reject the Chilean experience, promote the Brazilian and negotiate the Peruvian for essentially political as well as economic reasons; that changes in U.S. policy to Chile subsequent to the coup reflected the change in the political and economic orientations of the régimes; that U.S. military programmes and personnel complemented the activities of political and economic officials and contributed towards the same policy-goal; that U.S. policy contributed substantially and directly to the overthrow of the Allende Government.

The major thrust of this study is highly critical of the accounts minimising the role of the U.S. The socialist government of Chile represented the focal point of the new nationalist challenge to the United States in Latin America. Chile's tentative efforts to move out of the capitalist orbit and its support of ideological pluralism weakened the ties between the Northern and Southern hemisphere. It directly challenged U.S. political hegemony and the ability of U.S. policy makers to secure the continent economically for U.S. interests. Democratic socialism represented a systemic challenge, a conflict between two different modes of production.[6] U.S. policy makers refused to countenance nationalisation of U.S. economic assets in a country where *nationalisation was linked to a socialist, anticapitalist development strategy*. The overall U.S. response to the Allende government in Chile was twofold : a combination of severe economic pressures whose cumulative impact would result in internal economic chaos and a policy of disaggregating the Chilean state through creating ties with specific critical sectors (the military) and supporting their efforts at weakening the capacity of the state to realise a nationalist development project. This sustained policy of direct and indirect intervention culminated in a general societal crisis, a coup and a military government.

Entering the 1970's, the U.S. was faced with a new nationalist challenge in Latin America. A nationalist or regionalist front that emerged at the end of the 1960's could be divided into three distinct but interrelated groups : nationalist régimes (Bolivia, Peru and Chile); burgeoning nationalist movements (Uruguay and Argentina); and follower nations (Ecuador, Colombia, Venezuela and Panama). Within the group of 'leader' nationalist countries Chile, with its combined political and economic challenge to the U.S. based on mass popular participation, emerged as the core nation. To a lesser extent, the Bolivian government of General Torres represented a potential similar challenge. The Peruvian military junta, on the other hand, combined a policy of marginating large sectors of the population from effective participation in the political arena with an economic strategy designed to control and limit the access of foreign capital within a mixed economy. Nationalisations of foreign properties were interspersed with new concessions to foreign capital as the junta began to move, politically, to the right.

In Uruguay, a military-controlled civilian government moved decisively to weaken the electoral threat represented by the Frente Amplio and nationalist sectors of the political opposition. In Argentina, the anti-Marxism of Peron and the lack of significant foreign investment controls has been accompanied by a policy designed to crush the power of the nationalist left. The U.S. strategy of eliminating the nationalist threat in Chile, Bolivia and Uruguay, and increasing the pressures on Peru and Argentina has proved extremely successful. In order of vulnerability, the challenges in Bolivia and Uruguay were eliminated prior to the overthrow of the Allende government. In order of importance, however, Chile had priority status.

To understand the role played by the U.S. in the overthrow of the government of President Allende, it is important to consider the way in which the Chilean economy was dependent on the U.S. and its political system 'open' to U.S. influence. Chilean society, perhaps more than any other country in Latin America (on a per capita basis), was vegetating on 'borrowed time' or more specifically borrowed money. The standard of living of the heavily consumer oriented upper and middle class was not based on an expanding productive system but on foreign loans, credits and delayed payments. Throughout the sixties the foreign debt soared; and new loans chased after old debts in a spiraling sequence that left little investment for industrial expansion or agricultural growth. A historical analysis of Chile's increasing financial dependence during the decade preceding the Allende government is essential for measuring the impact of U.S. policies adopted after 1970. The dimensions of the problem of dependence include in general form :

1 the absolute size of the external debt, the payments schedule, the sources of re-financing.
2 the impact of the previous decades' loans in developing the productive capacity of the country to determine whether it generated new sources of capital for re-payments.
3 the sources of short-term credits and their impact on consumption and production.
4 impact of previous trade patterns on the problems of re-placement parts in strategic industrial-mineral-transport sectors.

Chilean economic dependence on the U.S. remained a significant factor during the period of the Allende government. U.S. direct private investment in Chile in 1970 stood at $1.1 billion,* out of a total estimated foreign investment of $1.672 billion.[7] Despite the diversification of investment in the 1960's—away from extractive industries and related service industries and towards manufacturing, trade and banking—the bulk of U.S. private investment in Chile remained in the mining and smelting sector (over 50 per cent). The balance was directed primarily into consumer-type activities and manufacturing.[8] However, U.S. and foreign corporations controlled almost all of the most dynamic and critical areas of the economy by the end of 1970 : machinery and equipment (50 per cent); iron, steel and metal products (60 per cent); petroleum products and distribution (over 50 per cent); industrial and other chemicals (60 per cent); rubber products (45 per cent); automotive assembly (100 per cent); radio and television (nearly 100 per cent); pharmaceuticals (nearly 100 per cent); office equipment (nearly 100 per cent); copper fabricating (100 per cent); tobacco (100 per cent); and advertising (90 per cent).[9] Furthermore, U.S. corporations controlled 80 per cent of the production of Chile's only

* Throughout this book 'billion' is used in the American sense, i.e. 'thousand million.'

important foreign exchange earner—copper. Hence, the Allende government was confronted with a situation of external control over copper production, technology and spare parts, and manufacturing, making the economy extremely vulnerable to financial and commercial pressures.

Although the level of Chile's imports from the U.S. declined from approximately 40 per cent of total imports during the Frei period to approximately 13 per cent in 1972, this quantitative decline in trade with the U.S. is deceiving because Chile continued to depend on the importation of essential replacement parts from North American firms. In addition, the precipitous decline in short-term U.S. commercial credits (from 78.4 per cent of the total in 1970 to approximately 6.6 per cent in 1972) seriously affected the Allende government's ability to purchase replacement parts and machinery for the most critical sectors of the economy—copper, steel, electricity, petroleum, and transportation. By late 1972, for example, it was estimated that almost one-third of the diesel trucks at Chuquicamata copper mine, 30 per cent of privately owned 'microbuses', 21 per cent of all taxibuses, and 33 per cent of state-owned buses in Chile (where the majority of buses and trucks originate from U.S. General Motors or U.S. Ford models) were unable to operate because of the lack of spare parts or tires. Over 90 per cent of spare parts in the copper industry were imported from the U.S. In overall terms, the value of U.S. machinery and transport equipment exported to Chile by U.S. firms declined from $152.6 million in 1970 to $110.0 million in 1971.[10]

Chile, probably more than most underdeveloped countries, was dependent on external financial sources to maintain month to month commercial operations as well as to finance so-called long-term development projects.

The export sector of the Chilean economy (mostly copper) was controlled, in part, by U.S. corporations; thus the main source of foreign exchange earnings was also controlled by U.S. firms. Production planning, marketing and sales were also under U.S. corporate control. About 95 per cent of the replacement parts for machinery in the copper industry were imported from the U.S. Given the high degree of integration that existed between the Chilean export sector and the U.S. economy, and given the Chilean economy's inordinate dependence on the export of copper for foreign exchange earnings to import crucial foodstuff, raw materials, parts, etc., externally induced abrupt and severe 'shocks' or 'dislocations' in the mining sector would have significant ramifications throughout the economy. The externally linked enclave in effect was a 'hostage' of the metropolitan countries: its high level technology and 'reach' into foreign markets made it highly vulnerable to actions and reactions in the metropolitan countries. The crucial theoretical point is that when countries evolve a pattern of development largely induced by external sources of finance, technology and machinery, and when they fail to develop out of the accumulated debts the productive capacity to satisfy debt obligations and new investment needs, a condition of vulnerability is engendered which makes the economy relatively easy to disrupt and highly susceptible to crisis. The points of foreign contact or entry, the transactions and exchanges that take place, become during the ensuing conflict points of access through which external groups can adversely affect the internal performance of the economy.

The first section of this book is a discussion of debt-accumulation in the period prior to the election of Salvador Allende. This discussion serves to highlight the non-developmental or political basis of loans and grants. In other words, the external debt not only becomes a political weapon once consummated, but from its very inception, during the process of debt accumulation, political ties between the U.S. and Chilean socio-political forces were primary considerations. The debt-basis of U.S.–Chilean relationships became the cause and consequence of the 'porous' nature of Chilean economic, social, and military institutions. The grants and loans resulted from commonly decided programmes based in intense interaction and mutual consultation between Chilean and U.S. officials. The externally linked channels of communication (as much as the networks themselves) devised to facilitate the transfer of funds became the points of access to Chilean decision-making and decision-makers.

The sudden and abrupt termination of external funds seriously disrupted the institutionally accepted mode of operation leaving a huge gap in the day-to-day operations of the economic system.

The combined impact of internal and external pressures began to affect Chilean production seriously after mid-1972 and increasingly thereafter :

Industrial Production in 1972[11]
(per cent change on 1971)

January	21.7
February	15.9
March	13.0
April	17.1
May	14.4
June	5.3
July	5.3
August	3.6
September	−8.7
October	−7.8
November	−8.1
December	−11.1

The downward trend in industrial production, as the table makes abundantly clear, begins with the mobilisation of the opposition and reaches a high point during the period of the intensification of opposition activity (September–December) designed to undermine the government's position.

Chile can be compared to a drug addict : daily injections of new foreign loans were necessary to nourish the 'habit' cultivated by previous régimes. The economy had lost the capacity to sustain itself on its own efforts. The 'rehabilitation' of the Chilean economy, given the extreme form of financial dependence on which it was found, would have required a painful shift of priorities that would have required at least a decade. . . . time and circumstances which were not available to the Allende Government. Short of a complete rupture in relations, a Government which attempts to reconstruct society, meet past financial obligations without continuing sources of funding, as well as operate through the established channels and networks will ultimately suffer dire economic and political consequences : the economic constraints will create severe internal bottlenecks and the political channels will serve to undermine the régime.

The second section of the paper deals with the decision-making structure that formulates U.S. policy. Contrary to the assertion of some commentators, the proliferation of policy-statements and action-proposals are not evidence of bureaucratic anarchy or the lack of any fixed policy-making centre. When the stakes at hand involve major challenges to the fundamental tenets of U.S. political economy (as was perceived to be the case in Chile) a centralised policy command was established, a 'general line' was elaborated, and a variety of policy-making agencies were delegated to implement a variety of complementary tasks derived from the general policy. The National Security Council formulated general policy which was transmitted to several governmental agencies (Treasury, CIA, State, Department of Defence) which in turn elaborated concrete measures which were then in turn put into practice 'in the field', whether it was Treasury appointees in the international banks, Central Intelligence Agency operatives infiltrating Chilean parties, or military advisors attached to the Chilean military command. The multiple dimensions of dependency and the porous nature of Chilean political, economic and social institutions facilitated successful implementation of many of the negative measures which the U.S. agencies formulated.

Private sector activity served to pressure government action and in turn responded to government policy-measures. The initiative taken by affected enterprises crystalised action by high policy-makers : once it became government policy to isolate the Allende Government, the private sector as a whole (commercial banks, firms, etc.) was mobilised and fell into line. The State was instrumental in converting the position of a fraction of the ruling class into the action of the class as a whole.

The specific U.S. policy responses to the Chilean effort at socialist transformation took several inter-related forms :

1 diplomatic and political pressure aimed at maximising international isolation of Chile.
2 economic squeeze to provoke economic dislocation and social conflict.
3 military aid to disaggregate the Chilean state, strengthen bonds between U.S. and Chilean military and lay the basis for a coup.
4 maintenance of political and diplomatic relations to collect information, maintain ties with political opposition, facilitate flow of financial resources to allies.

The negotiating posture simulated by U.S. officials in their dealings with their Chilean counterparts served to encourage the illusory hope among the Chileans that a long-term settlement was possible, which would lead to a re-opening of lines of credit, loans, etc. In light of the evidence which suggests that no such settlement was envisaged by U.S. policy-makers, we can conclude that the negotiations merely served as an information-gathering service : a means of measuring the relative strength of the régime, its capacity to resist pressure, its willingness to abandon positions, as well as to identify divisions within the government and to exploit them.

U.S. policy was not determined by any particular 'economic' decision in Chile, Latin America or the U.S. The overall policy of aggressive economic intervention articulated by the National Security Council and put in practice by U.S. agencies was derived from a commitment to oppose structural-ideological developments in Chile : the transformation of Chile into a democratic socialist society. The changes envisaged by the Allende Government not only restricted the capacity of U.S. capital to expand in Chile but threatened to dis-articulate the economic and trade patterns within the region. Changes in Chile potentially laid the basis for modifying and redefining Latin America's external economic relations. Under Allende Chile was still in transition, both in and out of the U.S. orbit and this accounts for its vulnerability to U.S. pressures.

U.S. policy to socialist countries or societies in transition to socialism varies according to the *porosity* of the state, the possibilities of reversing institutional changes and to the timing or consummation of transformation. Accordingly we can classify three different types of imperial strategies with three different types of socialist societies :

Type of State
1. Permeable state (Chile) : A state in which changes are reversible, sectors of state apparatus linked to old class structure and externally, political channels are open (parties, pressure groups, press, etc.).

Imperial Strategy
Maintain relations; disaggregate the state; avoid precipitous action that would lead to 'premature' rupture in relations, coalesce internal forces, contest external sources of funding. In the short run the notion is to maintain relations as a conduit for nourishing internal sources feeding into the disarticulated state and to avoid adverse polarisation (Nation *vs*. U.S.). The middle-range strategy is to prepare for a 'historic confrontation'—mobilising social

forces willing to reverse the institutional changes which have been brought into being : to dismantle and totally disaggregate the state. The strategic goal is to reconstitute the state in the image and the service of imperial foreign economic and diplomatic interests.

Type of State
2. Non-Permeable State ('Recent'—Cuba)
(In the imperial lexicon a 'totalitarian' state). A state in which *irreversible* changes have occurred—there being no possibility of disaggregating the *State* (for example, a popular militia has replaced the previous standing army), political channels are closed (parties and opposition pressure groups are disarticulated).
Imperial Strategy
Rupture relations, mount international campaign to 'isolate' target country, develop propaganda war focusing on 'closed nature' of society (which amounts to protest over loss of points of entry).

Type of State
3. Non-Permeable State (long-term—Soviet Union)
(Internal characteristics are similar to type two;) non-reversible changes, durable institutions, no points of access, etc.
Imperial Strategy
Possible accommodation ('co-existence'), re-open relations on basis of recognition of imperial spheres of influence; attempt long-term penetration of markets and obtain access to raw materials through loans and technological sales; short-term propaganda wars continue to explore internal differentiation.

Considering the situation of both the country in transition to socialism and the imperial country attempting to maintain its network, the possible choices open are quite limited. For the former the problem becomes one of rupturing relations at the historic moment when a maximum of internal forces can be polarised against the external enemy and their principal internal allies. The efforts by the Chilean Government to substitute tactical gains through negotiations was based on the mistaken and premature assumption of the possibility of co-existence between a permeable state and imperial country. For the latter, the maintenance of relations with Allende's Chile was an opportunity to reverse an increasingly socialised economy. By taking advantage of the multiple points of opposition permitted by the government, the U.S. channelled funds selectively to specific institutions (Army, Catholic University) which would serve as spearheads or points of support for the counter-revolution. Recipient institutions of external funding were sufficiently homogeneous in political composition to assure the donors that the funds would only strengthen the opposition. Covert subsidies promoted the mass activity tolerated by the government; these subsidies contributed in rapid succession to politicising, activising and mobilising substantial social forces leading to the creation of organisational focos which in turn captured the leadership of voluntary associations and disciplined the membership through a process of selective rewards and punishments. The subsidised and organised forces then focused their activities on the nerve centres of the economic infrastructure, transport and distribution. The armed forces entered the government to protect the social mobilisation of the opposition and increase the 'porosity' of the government. The military's penetration of government opened further channels for covert subsidies and subsequent activities became more audacious, causing government authority to crumble. The government was paralysed from within by subversive members of the state apparatus and undermined from the outside by the attacks on the 'nerves' of the economy.

Imperial policy is premised on the short-run need to dis-aggregate the state, disassemble critical institutions of the state apparatus and create commitments and loyalties to the interests of the external power. These social-political bonds facilitate the channelling back into the country, through the disarticulated state apparatus, the policies which will best serve them. This 'alienated' apparatus (serving external needs) subsequently dismantled or reshaped the institutions of the Allende government to serve their central political project: the reconstruction of a state apparatus as an instrument of private economic accumulation and expansion through mass repression. The whole of the state apparatus was re-made in the image of the alienated fragment. Hence the 'new state' can only be an alien state: the reconstructed state apparatus assumes the orientation of the disaggregated segment bound to the external power. From disaggregating the nation-state, the imperial country contributes to reconstructing and strengthening the state apparatus: homogeneous, centralised bodies linked at the top and extended outward to the metropolis emerge. In the language of imperial social science, the country has now reached the period of 'institution-building'.

Overall foreign economic relations are not only conditioned by political considerations, they frequently influence and shape them. In the context of considering the evolving U.S. foreign economic policies toward Chile, the crucial consideration for U.S. policy-makers was the elaboration of economic measures to consolidate or change (depending on the government) the class basis of state power and only secondarily to promote economic development or specific U.S. economic interests. The U.S. credit and trade squeeze was designed for a political purpose (not designed to serve specific economic interests) : to promote the political demise of a democratic socialist government. Economic pressures led to economic dislocation (scarcities) which generated the social basis (discontent among the lower middle class) that created the political context for a military coup. In a porous dependent society U.S. economic policy was a formidable instrument in shifting the internal balance of power against the change-oriented government. The inequalities in economic and military power between imperial and dependent countries once transferred into the sphere of internal struggles will tend to turn the balance against the anti-imperial forces. The Chilean experience suggests that only in the process of rupturing external relations and the concomitant closure of internal access points could the transition to socialism continue.

The separation of 'external' pressure from internal social struggles is inadequate for understanding the events in Chile or any other dependent country. Imperial induced shortages that adversely affected specific types of economic activities and/or social classes provoking social unrest and leading to political confrontations are indistinguishable from similar shortages caused by domestic wholesalers, distributors, etc. The 'external' forces were very much involved, even if their presence was not always physically visible. The yet unknown extent to which active agents of the U.S. penetrated political and social organisations is secondary to the fact that such activity complemented the larger economic pressures generated by activists based in the U.S.

NOTES

1 John H. Crimmins, Acting Assistant Secretary of State for Inter-American Affairs, before a House Foreign Affairs Subcommittee. See U.S. Congress, House, Committee on Foreign Affairs, Subcommittee on Inter-American Affairs, *United States–Chilean Relations*, 93rd Congress, 1st Session, March 6, 1973. Washington: U.S. Government Printing Office, 1973, p. 15.

2 Jack Kubisch, Assistant Secretary of State for Inter-American Affairs, before the House Foreign Affairs Committee, September 20, 1973. See *Department of State Bulletin*, October 8, 1973, pp. 465–466.

3 Henry Kissinger, Secretary of State, before the Senate Committee on Foreign Relations. See U.S. Congress, Senate, Committee on Foreign Relations, *Nomination of Henry A. Kissinger, Part 2* (Executive Hearings). Washington: U.S. Government Printing Office, 1973, p. 304.

4 Paul E. Sigmund, 'The "Invisible Blockade" and the Overthrow of Allende,' *Foreign Affairs*, January 1974, pp. 337–339.

5 Henry Landsberger, *Answers to Some Questions About the Military Coup in Chile*, unpublished paper, University of North Carolina at Chapel Hill, September 30, 1973, pp. 16, 22, 23, Appendix 3.

6 'Expropriation itself is an issue,' observed a National Security Council official, 'in that it bothers people domestically for ideological reasons.' *Interview No. 2–18*. National Security Council August 14, 1973.

7 Figures taken from a study prepared by CORFO in August 1972, as quoted from Kyle Steenland, 'Two Years of Popular Unity in Chile: a Balance Sheet,' *New Left Review*, March–April 1973, p. 14.

8. See James Petras & Robert LaPorte, Jr., 'U.S. Response to Economic Nationalism in Chile,' in James Petras, ed., *Latin America: From Dependence to Revolution*, New York: John Wiley & Sons, 1973, pp. 219–222.

9 See James D. Cockcroft, Henry Frundt, and Dale L. Johnson, 'The Multi-nationals,' in Dale L. Johnson, ed., *The Chilean Road to Socialism*. New York: Doubleday Anchor, 1973, p. 13.

10 'Chile: Facing the Blockade,' *NACLA's Latin American & Empire Report*, January 1973, pp. 20–21, 26–27; *Chile Hoy*, August 11–17, 1972, p. 16.

11 Economic Intelligence Unit, *Quarterly Economic Review of Chile*, No. 2, May 1973, p. 10.

CHAPTER I

The U.S. Role in Chile 1964-1970

There were several important events and experiences in Chilean political history during the six years prior to Allende's election which are critical to understanding the subsequent development of U.S.-Chilean relations : the role of the U.S. in the presidential elections of 1964; the extent and purpose of U.S. 'development' financing in Chile; and the impact of these efforts on Chilean development. The main conclusion is that U.S. political-economic involvement in Chile was successful in influencing short-run political events (electing Frei in 1964) but was a failure in its subsequent efforts to promote socio-economic development, thus setting the stage for a major political defeat, the election of Allende in 1970. The costs of U.S. economic involvement in Chilean politics, however, were shifted to the shoulders of the Chilean people after Allende was elected, in the form of a huge foreign debt. Hence we have the paradoxical result of the U.S. paying and winning, and then losing and collecting : external financing of development had more than one hidden advantage for the donor country.

Towards the end of the conservative Alessandri presidency (1958-1964), the U.S. government and U.S. corporations with large economic investments in Chile became increasingly concerned over a possible move to the left in the 1964 national elections. These fears were reinforced by the outcome of a special Congressional election in the traditionally conservative rural province of Curico in March 1964, where the vote for the left coalition (FRAP) candidate rose by over 10 per cent as compared to the 1963 results, while the Radical-Liberal-Conservative candidate's share of the vote declined by 17 per cent.[1] U.S. policy makers were initially divided over whether to support the presidential candidate of the right-wing Democratic Front, Julio Duran, or the leader of the Christian Democratic Party, Eduardo Frei. The CIA, high-level echelons of the State Department, and the U.S. Ambassador to Chile, Charles Cole, favoured

Duran, while most other influential policy makers within the Kennedy administration were oriented toward Frei. However, the Curico debacle had significant consequences for the upcoming presidential election. The Democratic Front disbanded, Duran withdrew his candidacy, and the Chilean right moved to support Frei. Within the U.S. government, a similar coalescence of support behind the candidacy of Eduardo Frei occurred. Frei's major opponent in the 1964 presidential election was the candidate of the FRAP coalition, Salvador Allende.

U.S. government and corporate intervention in the 1964 election on behalf of Frei took a number of forms. Approximately $20 million in U.S. funds was channelled into the Frei campaign, while at least 100 U.S. 'special personnel' were posted to Chile from Washington and other Latin American countries to engage in complementary activities.[2] 'U.S. government intervention in Chile in 1964 was blatant and almost obscene,' a key U.S. intelligence officer at the time recalled. 'We were shipping people off right and left, mainly State Department but also CIA with all sorts of covers.'[3] CIA overt operations took the form of subsidising—via conduits such as the International Development Foundation—peasant organisations or financing pro-Frei media operations. The State Department role was no less pervasive. An important U.S. policy-maker on Latin America at the time of the Chilean election distinguished between its public position and its contribution to an interventionist policy :

'The State Department maintained a façade of neutrality and proclaimed it from time to time . . . Individual officers—and economic counsellors—would look for opportunities. And where it was a question of passing money, forming a newspaper or community development programme, the operational people would do the work. AID found itself suddenly overstaffed, looking around for peasant groups or projects for slum dwellers . . . Once you established a policy of building support among peasant groups, government workers and trade unions, the strategies fell into place.'[4]

Executives of the U.S. copper companies in Chile also played an active role in the pre-election period. Indirectly, they bolstered Frei's position by accepting his programme of 'Chileanisation' of the copper industry as the only viable alternative to nationalisation. Moreover, 'Privately, top Washington officials admit Frei's election was greatly helped by the "serious efforts" of U.S. copper interests and the U.S. Information Agency.'[5]

An unusual influx of U.S. military personnel into Chile was also a characteristic of the period prior to the election. During 1963, an extra 45 U.S. military officers (over and above the 16 military attachés assigned to the U.S. Embassy) were posted to Chile and sent to various U.S. military missions around the country. A further delegation of 35 U.S. armed services officers arrived in the country approximately two or three months before the election. Coincidently, at the time of the election, the Chilean armed forces were engaged in 'anti-subversion exercises' and joint army-navy exercises were projected during the period when the Chilean Congress would be forced to vote for a new president if no candidate received an absolute majority of the total electoral vote.[6]

Between 1961 and 1970, Chile was the largest recipient of U.S. Alliance for Progress loans on a per capita basis of any country in Latin America—approximately $1.3 to $1.4 billion.[7] During the early years of the Alliance, the U.S. Agency for International Development (AID) justified substantial economic assistance to Chile on the basis of the country's 10-year development plan, even though the plan 'did not set forth clear priorities or definite projects. . . .' AID efforts to re-organise those sectors of the Chilean bureaucracy involved in the development process was 'ineffectual', and by the mid-1960's the attempt had 'virtually collapsed'. The structural problems of the Chilean government agencies were parallelled by the incapacity of AID to develop its own strategies for rational economic development. Aid evaluations of various Chilean government programmes and specific projects were 'inadequate' and 'provided little foundation for decisions in the way of objective research and analysis'.[8] Nevertheless, AID funds to Chile continued to increase, from $41.3 million in 1963 to $78.8 million to $99.5 million in 1965.[9]

By 1963, U.S. policy makers decided to change their strategy from making development assistance dependent upon structural administrative changes in the Chilean bureaucracy, to one of making it dependent 'upon Chile's accomplishing several narrowly defined fiscal and monetary goals aimed at stabilising domestic prices and effecting exchange reform'.[10] The aid disbursements for 1963, 1964, and 1965 were all essentially based on Chilean acceptance of fiscal and monetary stabilisation policies rooted in the adherence to yearly IMF 'standby' agreements. Yet the results were neither stabilisation nor development. The annual rate of inflation during 1963 and 1964 was 40 per cent (an increase over the two previous years), the trade deficit increased, and the economic growth rate declined. A Congressional study was severely critical of the U.S. government decision to attach the same conditions for the 1963 and 1964 AID disbursements, given the performance of the Chilean economy in 1963 as well as the unlikely event of structural economic reforms being implemented during an election year. The study concluded that the major rationale behind the programme was political—to bolster the position of the non-leftist forces in the 1964 presidential election :

'Clearly, the 1964 assistance package ($55 million programme loan; $15 million Export–Import Bank line of credit; $15 million Treasury exchange agreement) must have been based solely on political considerations—to maintain Chile's current levels of economic activity and investment and to support the balance of payments so that financial deterioration and unemployment would not occur in an election year.'[11]

Total assistance to Chile from the U.S. government was actually far in excess of the above figures. In this respect, it is interesting to note the expenditure levels over the three-year period, 1963 to 1965. Overall aid increased dramatically from $97.7 million in 1963 to $260.4 million in 1964, and then decreased just as rapidly to $92.5 million in 1965.[12] The 1964 allocation included a $40 million general economic development grant to alleviate the unemployment situation. 'We did not want to have a condition of vast unemployment as Chile was going into the election,' recalled a former AID official.[13] Another example of the political nature of the aid allocation in 1964 was a $15 million loan in May for commodity imports because of a U.S. 'desire to dampen the inflation in the pre-election period by financing additional imports. . . .'[14]

AID continued to push for increased and disproportionate economic assistance to Chile throughout the 1960's. As a predecessor to OPIC, AID also issued $1.8 billion in political risk insurance in Chile during the 1965 to 1970 period. A study prepared for the House Foreign Affairs Committee concluded that this insurance was 'part of U.S. policy to help support the government of Eduardo

Frei's Christian Democratic Party, although no ratified bilateral agreement existed between the two governments.'[15] One AID official involved in this activity recounted that in the last three months of 1967, 'everyone was pushing us to issue as much insurance in Chile as we could.'[16]

The AID presentation to Congress for increased financial appropriations for Chile in fiscal 1971—made just prior to the 1970 election—was accompanied by a recognition on the agency's part 'that the Alliance had failed dismally in its objectives in this country. . . .'[17] The inflation rate in 1969 was the highest since Frei took office; government policies in the agricultural sector (land reform, per capita production, etc.) had failed visibly; and the growth rate of the gross national product for the period 1965–1969 compared unfavourably with the period 1961–1965.[18]

The Frei government was also the recipient of substantial amounts of development assistance in the form of loans and grants from U.S. government banks and U.S.-influenced international financial institutions. The U.S. Export-Import Bank made loans totalling $254.4 million to Chile between 1967 and 1969. The World Bank and the Inter-American Development Bank were also active. Between 1965 and 1970, the loans to Chile by each institution amounted to $98 million and $192.1 million, respectively.[19] By December 1970, Chile had accumulated a public and private debt of $3.83 billion dollars, most of it owed to U.S. government agencies and private lenders.

As the evidence of congressional hearings and testimony, interviews and news accounts indicate, U.S. economic policy was politically motivated : directed at promoting an anti-socialist candidate, government and policies and preventing a socialist from succeeding. The heavy direct and indirect financial subsidies of the Frei candidacy and later presidency against Allende and the Left by the U.S. government and corporations, and the joint military activities were early indications of the policies that the U.S. would adopt during the Allende presidency. Only then the process was reversed : loans to the government were cut off, aid was channelled to the military and covert funding was directed to opposition groups. The combined efforts of private and public officials in favour of Frei and against Allende in 1964 continued (with some modifications) with the election of Allende. The continuity of U.S. policy, its opposition to the Left before Allende came to power, makes untenable the argument that Allende's specific policy measures were responsible for U.S. policy. Both during the 1960's and 1970's there is a consistent pattern in U.S. policy of active involvement in support of U.S. economic and political interests, utilising loans, credits, subsidies and military programmes. U.S. economic involvement contributed to the election of Eduardo Frei in 1964 (though it was insufficient to prevent Allende's victory in 1970) and to the downfall of Allende in September 1973. The U.S. is an active, partisan participant in the major internal political struggles in Chile utilising its economic resources in an effort to buttress its political and class allies through electoral contests when possible, through military means when necessary.

NOTES

1 Federico G. Gil, *The Political System of Chile*, Boston: Houghton Mifflin Co., 1966, p. 242–243.
2 Laurence Stern, 'U.S. Helped Beat Allende in 1964,' *Washington Post*, April 6, 1973, p. A1, A12.
3 Quoted in *ibid*.
4 Quoted in *ibid*. According to an I.T.T. memorandum, 'The U.S. government sponsored and paid for special political polls, analysed Frei's campaign, gave him extraordinary consolation and comfort all under the friendly aegis of then U.S. Ambassador Ralph Dungan.' See U.S. Congress, Senate, Committee on Foreign Relations, Subcommittee on Multinational Corporations, *Multinational Corporations and United States Foreign Policy*, Part 2, 93rd Congress, March 20, 21, 22, 27, 28, 29, and April 4, 1973. Washington: U.S. Government Printing Office, 1973, p. 704.
5 Quoted in David J. Morris, *We Must Make Haste Slowly: The Process of Revolution in Chile*, New York: Vintage Books, 1973, p. 56.
6 See Miles D. Wolpin, *Cuban Foreign Policy and Chilean Politics*, Lexington, Mass.: D. C. Heath & Co., 1972, p. 92.
7 U.S. Congress, House, Committee on Banking and Currency, *Latin American Economic Study*, 91st Congress, 1st Session, October 1969. Washington: U.S. Government Printing Office, 1969, p. 19; U.S. Congress, Senate, Committee on Foreign Relations, Subcommittee on Multinational Corporations, *Multinational Corporations and United States Foreign Policy*, Part 1, 93rd Congress, March 20, 21, 22, 27, 28, 29 and April 4, 1973. Washington: U.S. Government Printing Office, 1973, p. 113.
8 U.S. Congress, Senate, Committee on Government Operations, Subcommittee on Foreign Aid Expenditures, *United States Foreign Aid*

in Action: A Case Study, 89th Congress, 2nd Session, Washington: U.S. Government Printing Office, 1966, pp. 50–51.

9   U.S. Congress, House, Committee on Foreign Affairs, *Development Assistance to Latin America 1961–1970*, April 14, 1971, Committee Print. Washington: U.S. Government Printing Office, 1971, pp. 9–10 (Tables 9 & 19).

10 U.S. Congress, Senate, *United States Foreign Aid in Action: A Case Study*, op. cit., p. 103.

11 *Ibid.*, p. 106. In a post-election audit, AID also found that between $60,000 and $70,000 worth of U.S. food supplies donated to CARITAS (the major social welfare agency of the Catholic Church in Chile) had been 'diverted to Christian Democratic campaigners during the campaign.' See Miles D. Wolpin, op. cit., p. 345.

12 Harvey S. Perloff, *Alliance for Progress*, Baltimore, Maryland: Johns Hopkins Press, 1969, p. 230 (Table A–3).

13 Quoted in Laurence Stern, op. cit. Also see, Jerome Levinson and Juan de Onis, *The Alliance That Lost Its Way*, Chicago: Quadrangle Books, 1972, p. 91.

14 Joan M. Nelson, *Aid, Influence, and Foreign Policy*, New York: Macmillan Co., 1968, p. 99.

15 U.S. Congress, House, Committee on Foreign Affairs, *The Overseas Private Investment Corporation*, 93rd Congress, 1st Session, Committee Print, September 4, 1973. Washington: U.S. Government Printing Office, 1973, p. 95.

16 Quoted in *ibid.*

17 'Excerpts from AID's Presentation of the Case for Increased Aid to Chile in the Months Preceding Allende's Election,' *Inter-American Economic Affairs*, Winter 1970, p. 91. AID requested a $9.3 million increase in aid over the 1970 authorisation.

18 *Ibid.*, p. 91.

Chile: Annual Growth Rates of GDP, 1961–1969 (%)

1961	*1962*	*1963*	*1964*	*1965*	*1966*	*1967*	*1968*	*1969*
6.2	5.0	4.7	4.2	5.0	7.0	2.3	2.9	3.3

See Organisation of American States, Inter-American Economic and Social Council, Inter-American Committee on the Alliance for Progress, *Domestic Efforts and Needs for External Financing for the Development of Chile*, CIAP Subcommittee on Chile, April 24–28, 1972, Washington, D.C., OEA/Ser.H/XIV, CIAP/541, April 21, 1972, p. 102.

19 See Agency for International Development, *U.S. Overseas Loans and Grants and Assistance from International Organisations*, Obligations and Loan Authorisations, July 1, 1945–June 30, 1972. Published May 1973, pp. 42, 181.

CHAPTER II

U.S. Policy and the Election of Allende: September - November 1970

Having failed in their efforts to influence the elections through financial subsidies to the non-socialist candidates, U.S. policy-makers, CIA and private corporate officials were thrown in disarray with the victory of Allende. Kissinger and his foreign policy advisors were forced to improvise policy within very limited time constraints and with few immediate prospects. The initial response was one of defining the political situation resulting from the election. Kissinger's definition of political reality included three elements: (1) maximum priority was assigned to Chilean political developments, (2) Chile was specified as a maximum danger area within the region; (3) political developments in the region were linked to the evolution of events in Chile.

Hence for U.S. policy-makers the political situation in Chile was of strategic importance to the possible relations which would develop between the U.S. and Latin America.

The confusion which reigned among U.S. private and public officials resulted in the absence, initially, of a coordinated and combined effort. The State Department sought to influence Christian Democrats and parliamentarians to vote against the confirmation of Allende. The Ambassador, while supporting those efforts, also maintained contact with the International Telephone and Telegraph Corporation and took other initiatives. The ITT proposed more aggressive direct intervention by the U.S. government, offered subsidies to the CIA, pressured the Ambassador and favoured efforts directed toward an immediate overthrow. The CIA established contacts with the banking and corporate world hoping to precipitate an economic crisis which would force the Christian Democrats to deny Allende the presidency. This multi-prong economic strategy did not prevent the CIA from developing contacts with the Chilean military which, however, was not politically and organisationally prepared for a coup. The precipitous efforts of ITT predicated on the possibility of an immediate coup came into conflicts with the efforts of the CIA which apparently favoured a policy of creating more propitious political conditions for a military coup. The element of miscalculation and surprise and the improvisation of policy measures failed to prevent Allende from taking office.

The U.S. government and various U.S. corporations with extensive economic interests in Chile expressed considerable interest in influencing the outcome of the Chilean presidential election prior to September. In anticipation of a possible victory by Salvador Allende and the Unidad Popular, a series of meetings took place in May/June 1970 between ITT director and former head of the CIA, John A. McCone, and the then CIA director Richard Helms. Their discussions centred around the question of how the U.S. government could actively support the candidacy of either of Allende's opponents, Conservative Jorge Alessandri or Christian Democrat Radomiro Tomic. On June 4, this topic was discussed at a specially convened meeting of the U.S. government's interdepartmental 'Forty Committee' which is responsible for approving covert CIA global operations. The meeting was chaired by the President's national Security Advisor, Henry Kissinger.[1] Although a full account of the proceedings is not yet available the Committee authorised a CIA plan to use $400,000 in support of anti-Allende media activities during the election campaign. It is conceivable that other activities were ruled out until after the election, because the U.S. Embassy in Chile—on the basis of a series of polls carried out by the CIA—was predicting an Alessandri plurality of approximately 40 per cent of the popular vote.[2]

The initial U.S. government response to Allende's success was one of shock and hostility. The Nixon Adminstration immediately began to make efforts to block his confirmation by voicing fears that Allende as president would eventually culminate in a Communist government in Chile, and raised the spectre of similar developments occurring in Argentina, Peru, and Bolivia. The 'Forty Committee' held an urgent meeting to discuss the implications of the Chilean results for U.S. policy and to plan counter-moves. In Chile, U.S. Ambassador Edward Korry drafted a memorandum to the State Department containing a negative assessment of the Allende victory and its long-term consequence : 'I said that over the course of six years there would be an irreversible political structure (in Chile) . . .'³ Henry Kissinger, the President's National Security Council Advisor, played a key role in formulating the general contours of U.S. policy towards a socialist Chile. In a White House briefing on September 16, he described Allende as 'probably a Communist' who represented 'a non-democratic party, which tends to make his election pretty irreversible.' Kissinger suggested that an Allende presidency would signal the end of open electoral politics in Chile and argued that a Communist Chile would have a direct impact on the future direction of Argentina ('which is already deeply divided'), Peru ('which has already been heading in directions that have been difficult to deal with') and Bolivia ('which has also gone in a more leftist, anti-U.S. direction'). The problem was global and hemispheric, but the transformation of policy goals into concrete policy actions would require a more favourable conjuncture of events than existed :

'. . . I don't think we should delude ourselves that an Allende takeover in Chile would not present massive problems for us, and for democratic forces and for pro-U.S. forces in Latin America, and indeed to the whole Western Hemisphere. What would happen to the Western Hemisphere Defence Board, or to the Organisation of American States, and so forth, is extremely problematical. So we are taking a close look at the situation. It is not one in which our capacity for influence is very great at this particular moment now that matters have reached this particular point.'⁴

A Congressional study was led to observe that 'it is, accordingly, clear that both the U.S. Embassy in Santiago and high levels of the U.S. government in Washington viewed with hostility the prospects of an Allende government.'⁵ This hostility was the basis of U.S. policy efforts to overthrow the Allende government.

The U.S. business community responded similarly, speaking of 'the serious implications of Allende's ascension to power for the United States and United States business.'⁶ One multinational corporation with substantial economic assets in Chile—International Telephone and Telegraph—decided on a concerted policy aimed at preventing Allende's inauguration as president. With the active support of the U.S. government, they hoped to reinstate a government supportive of the status quo and U.S. investor interests in Chile. Beginning in mid-1970, ITT officials proceeded to establish contact within the National Security Council, the State Department ('We maintained daily and almost hourly communications with State as regards Chile,' wrote ITT senior vice-president, Edward Gerrity), the United States Information Agency, the Overseas Private Investment Corporation, the Central Intelligence Agency, the Inter-American Development Bank, the Senate Foreign Relations Committee, and the House Foreign Affairs Committee. Furthermore, their relationships with U.S. Embassy personnel in Chile were close and long-standing : 'During Ambassador Korry's visit to Washington we always conferred with him. We have close relationships with various officers of the Santiago Embassy and we have conferred with them both in Washington and in Santiago.'[7]

Immediately after the September election, an ITT official contacted Kissinger's senior advisor on Latin America, Viron Vaky, to inform him that ITT was prepared to support financially any U.S. government plan to prevent Allende's inauguration as president by the Chilean Congress :

'I told Mr Vaky to tell Mr Kissinger Mr Geneen (ITT Chairman) is willing to come to Washington to discuss ITT's interest and that we are prepared to assist financially in sums up to seven figures. I said Mr Geneen's concern is not one of "after the barn door has been locked," but that all along we have feared the Allende victory and have been trying unsuccessfully to get other American companies aroused over the fate of their investments and join us in pre-election efforts.'[8]

Meanwhile, U.S. Ambassador Korry (according to an ITT memorandum) was actively engaged in the effort to thwart an Allende presidency :

'Late Tuesday night (September 15) Ambassador Edward Korry finally received a message from State Department giving him the green light to move in the name of President Nixon. The message gave him maximum authority to do all possible—short of a Dominican Republic-type action—to keep Allende from taking power.

'Ambassador Korry, before getting a go-signal from Foggy Bottom, clearly put his head on the block with his extremely strong message to State. He also, to give him due credit, started to manoeuvre with the Christian Democratic, the Radical and National parties and other Chileans—without State authorisation —immediately after the election results were known. He has never let up on Frei to the point of telling him to "put his pants on".'[9]

On September 29, CIA director Richard Helms instructed the head of the Clandestine Services Western Hemisphere Division of the CIA, William V. Broe, to arrange a meeting with ITT vice-president Edward Gerrity:

Senator Church. 'Did you discuss with Mr Gerrity the feasibility of possible actions by U.S. companies designed to create or accelerate economic instability in Chile?'

Mr Broe. 'I explored with Mr Gerrity the feasibility of possible actions to apply some economic pressure on Chile; yes, sir.'

Senator Church. 'What did you understand the purpose of applying economic pressure to be?'

Mr Broe. 'Well, at that time, September 29, the Christian Democratic Members of Congress were showing indications of swinging their full support to Allende in the belief that they could make a political bargain with him. . . . At the same time, the economic situation had worsened because of the reaction to the Allende election, and there were indications that this was worrying the Christian Democratic Congressmen. There was a thesis that additional deterioration in the economic situation could influence a number of Christian Democratic Congressmen who were planning to vote for Allende. This is what was the thesis.'

Senator Church. 'This was the purpose then. Did you discuss with Mr Gerrity the feasibility of banks not renewing credits or delaying in doing so?'

Mr Broe. 'Yes, sir.'

Senator Church. 'Did you discuss with Mr Gerrity the feasibility of companies dragging their feet in spending money and making deliveries and in shipping spare parts?'

Mr Broe. 'Yes, I did.'

Senator Church. 'Did you discuss with Mr Gerrity the feasibility of creating pressure on saving and loan institutions in Chile so that they would have to shut their doors, thereby creating stronger pressure?'

Mr Broe. 'Yes.'
Senator Church. 'Did you discuss with Mr Gerrity the feasibility of withdrawing all technical help and not promising any technical assistance in the future?'
Mr Broe. 'Yes, sir.'[10]

The decision of a significant number of Christian Democratic Congressmen to support Allende's confirmation as President, and thus virtually guarantee his election, necessitated prolonging the application of these economic measures. The goals of the CIA and ITT shifted : economic pressures no longer were directed at convincing recalcitrant Christian Democratic Congressmen but at activating the military to intervene in political life.

An ITT memorandum from field operatives in Chile, noting the strength of Allende's congressional support, described the more 'pragmatic' option :

'A more realistic hope among those who want to block Allende is that a swiftly deteriorating economy (bank runs, plant bankruptcies, etc.) will touch off a wave of violence resulting in a military coup . . . Chances of thwarting Allende's assumption of power now are pegged mainly to an economic collapse which is being encouraged by some sectors of the business community and by President Frei himself.'[11]

After Allende was assured of congressional confirmation, CIA activities were directed towards encouraging a military takeover by the Chilean armed forces as the remaining viable option. John McCone summarised a meeting at CIA headquarters with William Broe : 'Approaches continue to be made to select members of the Armed Forces in an attempt to have them lead some sort of uprising —no success to date.'[12] A subsequent ITT memorandum raised the issue of direct U.S. government involvement in a coordinated coup attempt, at the *propitious moment* :

'It is a fact that word was passed to Viaux from Washington to hold back last week. It was felt that he was not adequately prepared, his timing was off, and he should 'cool it' for a later, unspecified date. Emissaries point out to him that if he moved prematurely and lost, his defeat would be tantamount to a "Bay of Pigs in Chile." As part of the persuasion to delay, Viaux was given oral assurance he would receive material assistance and support from the U.S. and others for a later manoeuvre.'[13]

Realising that the presidency in Chile would pass to a socialist in November, ITT officials began to elaborate a strategy of external economic coercion designed to lead to internal economic chaos and the ultimate demise of the new government. ITT Chairman Geneen now emphasised that company officials in contact with U.S. government representatives 'should demand that U.S. representatives of international banks take a strong stand against any loan to countries expropriating American companies or discriminating against foreign private capital.'[14] This strategy was outlined in more detail in an ITT analysis of U.S. policy toward Latin America submitted to Henry Kissinger in late October :

'Inform President Allende that, if his policy requires expropriation of American property, the United States expects speedy compensation in U.S. dollars or convertible foreign currency as required by international law.

'Inform him that in the event speedy compensation is not forthcoming, there will be immediate repercussions in official and private circles. This could mean a stoppage of all loans by international banks and U.S. private banks.

'Continue the foregoing trend with every possible pressure which might keep Dr Allende within bounds. . . .

'Without informing President Allende, all U.S. aid funds already committed to Chile should be placed in the "under review" status in order that entry of money into Chile is temporarily stopped with a view to a permanent cut-off if necessary. This includes "funds in the pipeline"—"letters of credit" or any such.'[15]

This strategy was ultimately incorporated into U.S. government policy and became central to the attainment of U.S. policy goals in Chile.[16]

After a period in which U.S. corporations and government officials appeared to be working at cross purposes and without a clear political perspective (except their desire to undermine the election of Allende) a consensus emerged between Kissinger, CIA, ITT. The convergence of views was reached shortly after Allende was confirmed in the presidency : by common consent the strategy consisted of maximising external economic pressures on the vulnerable points of the Chilean economy, creating political conditions for a coup within a time span longer than what was originally envisaged by the early opponents of Allende.

NOTES

1 U.S. Congress, Senate, Committee on Foreign Relations, Subcommittee on Multinational Corporations, *The International Telephone and Telegraph Company and Chile, 1970–71,* Committee Print, June 21, 1973, 93rd Congress. Washington: U.S. Government Printing Office, 1973, p. 3.

2 U.S. Congress, Senate, Committee on Foreign Relations, Subcommittee on Multinational Corporations, *Multinational Corporations and United States Foreign Policy, Part 1,* op. cit., p. 290.

3 *Ibid.,* pp. 291–292. A high-level Treasury Department official described the 1970 elections as 'a presumably democratic type of election.' *Interview No. 2–17:* Washington, D.C., August 13, 1973.

4 U.S. Congress, Senate, Committee on Foreign Relations, Subcommittee on Multinational Corporations, *Multinational Corporations and United States Foreign Policy, Part 2,* op. cit., pp. 542–543. Also see, Tad Szulc, 'Briefing on Chile Disturbs Chile,' *New York Times,* September 23, 1970, p. 13.

5 U.S. Congress, Senate, *The International Telephone and Telegraph Company and Chile 1970–71,* op. cit., p. 9.

6 'Business in Chile Braces for Storm After Election Victory by Marxist Allende,' *Business Latin America,* September 10, 1970, p. 290.

7 U.S. Congress, Senate, *Multinational Corporations and United States Foreign Policy, Part 2, op. cit.,* pp. 801–803.

8 *Ibid.,* pp. 599–600. Similar information was also conveyed to Charles Meyer, Assistant Secretary of State for Inter-American Affairs. According to McCone, the original directive from ITT chairman Harold S. Geneen was quite specific :

> 'What he told me at that time was that he was prepared to put as much as a million dollars in support of any plan that was adopted by the government for the purpose of bringing about a coalition of the opposition to Allende so that when confirmation was up, which was some months later, this coalition would be united and deprive Allende of his position.'
> *Ibid., Part 1,* p. 102.

ITT memoranda were highly critical of the refusal of other U.S. corporations with economic interests in Chile to support ITT's policy :

> 'Repeated calls to firms such as GM, Ford, and banks in California and New York have drawn no offers of help. All have some sort of excuse.' *Ibid., Part 2,* p. 643.
> 'Practically no progress has been made in trying to get American

business to cooperate in some way so as to bring on economic chaos.'
Ibid., p. 644.

This division, however, was essentially short-term and a question of tactics rather than policy. A number of U.S. corporations were prepared to withhold action until after the results of compensation negotiations with the Allende Government for any expropriated properties.

9 *Ibid.*, pp. 608–609.
10 *Ibid., Part 1*, pp. 250–251.
11 *Ibid., Part 2*, p. 622.
12 *Ibid.*, p. 644.
13 *Ibid.*, p. 659. Ex-General Viaux was convicted of conspiring in the assassination of the constitutionalist Commander-in-Chief of the Chilean armed forces, General Pene Schneider, in October 1970.
14 *Ibid.*, pp. 665–666.
15 *Ibid.*, pp. 720–721.
16 U.S. policy-makers distinguished between the more 'neanderthal' aspects of ITT's strategy (e.g. 'public threats') and those aspects such as economic coercion which were more in line with the new 'low profile' policy. *Interview No. 2–16*: Washington, August 9, 1973.

CHAPTER III

The National Security Council and the Initial U.S. Response to Allende

The election of Salvador Allende and the apparent inability of the U.S. to prevent that outcome was a signal to the Nixon administration of the inadequacy of the foreign policy making apparatus. For the U.S. Executive viewed events in Chile as inextricably bound to development throughout the region and a direct challenge to U.S. hegemony, already eroded in countries adjoining Chile. Nixon's first response was a statement which outlined his concern with 'coherence' and 'rationality' in formulating policy toward the region : the multitude of U.S. private economic and political interests had to be brought into order. To correct the organisational deficiencies and to provide the coherence in policy which he sought several organisational changes were instituted, leading to the formation of a centralised policy-making body capable of coordinating the various threads of U.S. policy. The National Security Council emerged as the crucial policy-making body. It assumed responsibility for devising Chilean policy; and it quickly became apparent that a policy of *political* confrontation was chosen. The particular issues raised, including nationalisation and compensation, were symptomatic of a larger issue : the effort by Chile to break its ties with the U.S. and seek an alternative to capitalist development. It was that decision and the U.S. opposition which defined the operational meaning of the 'political' problem, frequently referred to by high NSC officials, including Kissinger.

In his 1970 foreign policy report to the U.S. Congress, President Nixon dwelled on the need for a special decision-making instrument to deal with critical foreign policy issues and to integrate them into the larger context of long-term U.S. global interests :

'American foreign policy must not be merely the result of a series of piecemeal tactical decisions forced by the pressure of events. If our policy is to embody a coherent vision of the world and a rational conception of America's interests, our specific actions must be the products of rational and deliberate choice. We need a system which forces consideration of problems before they become emergencies, which enables us to make our basic determinations of purpose before being pressed by events, and to mesh policies.'[1]

Such an instrument had been in the making since the beginning of the Administration, when the decision was made to revive the power of the National Security Council in order that it might 'set forth the major foreign policy problems facing the President, discuss the options available to him, and recommend courses of action.'[2] A Presidential aide described the broad purpose of the Council as one of 'anticipat(ing) crises and organis(ing) options in advance of crises.'[3] As a result the 'responsibility for coordinating foreign planning' passed from Secretary of State William Rogers to the President's adviser on national security affairs and head of the National Security Council, Henry Kissinger.[4]

A series of executive department changes enhanced the stature of the National Security Council in the area of foreign policy and consolidated Kissinger's position as the President's most influential foreign policy adviser. In late 1969, Kissinger was appointed chairman of the newly-created Defence Programmes Review Committee 'whose purpose is to keep the annual defence budget in line with foreign policy objectives.'[5] This decision led to a serious weakening of the Secretary of Defence's previously dominant influence over interdepartmental discussions regarding the defence budget. According to a senior Pentagon planner, 'the consultation process (was) being formalised and broadened . . . with Henry Kissinger placed in the key post of deciding which issues must be resolved by the President himself.'[6] Kissinger was also appointed chairman of two key interdepartmental committees: the 'Forty Committee' which supervises covert U.S. intelligence operations around the world; and the Senior Review Group which 'usually gives final approval to the NSC study memoranda . . .'[7] In addition, Kissinger chairs the NSC 'Washington Special Actions Group' which is 'the top-level operations centre for sudden crises and emergencies . . .'[8] In 1971, a special intelligence committee under National Security Council leadership was established by President Nixon to review and evaluate global intelligence reports.[9] Hence, Kissinger and the National Security Council were assigned a central role in the shaping of military and intelligence policy as it impinges on overall foreign policy objectives.

Kissinger's immediate response to the Allende electoral victory in September 1970 was to estimate its impact on the hemisphere and to view it as a direct challenge to U.S. economic and political interests in Latin America. He assigned Chile priority status and implied that a short-term or prolonged confrontation between the U.S. and a socialist government in Chile was inevitable. An NSC official described the fundamental difference between the U.S. government assessment of Chile and Peru :

'The pattern was not that different with regard to nationalisation . . . The important difference is that in the Peruvian context you had a different political context. U.S. policy toward Chile was considered entirely within a much larger political context and was more important in a political sense, and was determined to a large extent by political factors.

'In the case of Peru, there was a non-constitutional government and policy was largely determined by the IPC dispute. The copper expropriations were a major factor in Chile, but our relations were still determined by political factors. When Nixon and Kissinger assessed Chile after the 1970 election, they were not looking at it primarily in terms of the expropriation of U.S. copper companies.'[10]

On November 4, 1970, Salvador Allende was inaugurated as the new president of Chile. The Popular Unity government described Chile as 'a dependency of imperialism' and proposed replacing 'the present economic structure, putting an end to the power of monopolistic capital, both Chilean and foreign, and also to big landowners, so as to begin the construction of socialism.'[11]

The U.S. reaction was 'brusque and frigid,'[12] barely concealing an open hostility. President Nixon outlined the basis of future U.S.-Chilean relations in his foreign policy report to Congress in February 1971 :

'We deal with governments as they are. Our relations depend not on their internal structures or social systems, but on actions which affect us and the inter-American system.

'The new government of Chile is a clear case in point. The 1970 election of a socialist president may have profound implications not only for its people but for the inter-American system as well. The government's legitimacy is not in question, but its ideology is likely to influence its actions. Chile's decision to establish ties with Communist Cuba, contrary to the collective policy of the OAS, was a challenge to the inter-American system . . .

'Our bilateral policy is to keep open the lines of communication. We will not be the ones to upset traditional relations . . . In short, we are prepared to have the kind of relationship with the Chilean government that it is prepared to have with us.'[13]

Disquiet was expressed in some U.S. Congressional quarters over the possible 'outright discrimination' by the Chilean government against U.S. corporate holdings in Chile.[14]

U.S. policy-makers envisaged a definite erosion of U.S.–Chilean relations in the immediate future. A senior U.S. policy adviser on Latin America recalled the atmosphere within U.S. government circles at the time, and the early application of direct and indirect economic pressures against the Allende government :

'The election of Allende came as something of a surprise. People didn't really believe it would happen. I think there was a fairly strong reaction to that election in the White House. The concept of a Marxist freely elected. . . . The approach taken was essentially to try to keep hands off as much as possible, but we certainly weren't interested in being terribly helpful to the success of the Allende government . . . Correct but cool. But the expectation was that there would be problems because of the kinds of people in the coalition, the programme of the coalition, the kinds of statements made, and the clear intention of nationalising the copper industry.

'Our policy was (characterised) increasingly by a growing resentment of economic nationalism, and a feeling that we couldn't ignore this. But even with Chile, an attempt was made to keep the lines open. Feeling that it was at least probable that economic pressures building up because of our economic policies and limited access to international agencies would either force Allende to compromise or, alternately, bring about some change in Chile.'[15]

U.S. corporations with investment interests in Chile increased their activity during this initial period. Under the aegis of ITT, an Ad Hoc Committee on Chile was formed to apply pressure on the U.S. government 'wherever possible to make it clear that a Chilean takeover (of their investments) would not be tolerated without serious repercussions following.'[16] The major focus of their efforts was Henry Kissinger and the National Security Council, and secondarily, within the U.S. Congress. ITT officials were in direct contact with Kissinger's office during January/February 1971 through the person of NSC official Arnold Nachmanoff. According to ITT documents, Nachmanoff, a senior Latin American adviser to Kissinger, told ITT officials that 'the best way to get at Chile is through her economy' and 'indicated that the U.S. will apply quiet pressure along economic lines and encourage other countries not to invest in Chile.'[17] At the initial Ad Hoc Committee meeting in January 1971, it was also argued that 'pressure should be brought upon the international lending agencies to cease activity in countries that threaten or actually expropriate private investments whether it is overtly or by "creeping nationalisation".'[18] ITT representatives at the meeting suggested that the 'threat of economic chaos'[19] would have a positive impact on Allende's attitude toward the problems of U.S. corporations in Chile.

The future course of relations between the United States and Chile was clear as early as February 1971. A group of Chilean government officials, headed by the Minister of the Economy, Pedro Vuskovic, visited Washington to argue Chile's case for continued public and private U.S. investment. In the course of discussions, senior U.S. government officials underlined the importance of adequate compensation for expropriated foreign properties. This reflected 'the strong pressure on the Administration by United States mining and other private interests whose total investment in Chile (is) estimated at more that $1 billion . . .'[20] At approximately the same time, President Nixon, with State Department support and at the urging of National Security Adviser Kissinger, cancelled a proposed visit of the U.S. aircraft carrier, Enterprise, to Chile. Kissinger supposedly argued that the visit would be viewed as a gesture of friendship by the U.S. toward a Marxist president.[21]

In Chile this decision was criticised by the right-wing opposition who saw the necessity of maintaining close and friendly ties between U.S. military forces and their Chilean counterparts as an essential ingredient in the formula to topple the Allende government. Subsequently the U.S. government 'rectified' this tactical error and encouraged military aid, joint exercises and a substantial U.S. military mission in Chile.

Summary

The National Security Council in consultation and cooperation with an association of large U.S. corporations collaborated in the coordination of a medium-range political strategy to undermine the Allende government. Through their combined efforts they determined the closure of vital financial and economic resources necessary to sustain Chile's dependent economy. The U.S. policy-makers' association with the corporate community and their ability to fashion a common policy was not a fortuitous coincidence but largely reflects the common interests that both share in maintaining Chile within the U.S. sphere of influence. The effort to centralise and rationalise the decision-making structure coincided with the crises in Chilean–U.S. relations and the inadequacy of piece-meal improvised policy responses. By organisational rationalisation an effort was made to get on top of events, and to anticipate and shape their direction. The constraints and options that U.S. policy-makers faced in devising a policy for Chile were not only dictated by developments in Chile but by the course of events in the region and especially in Peru and Brazil which in different ways influenced the policy choices of U.S. decision-makers.

NOTES

1   Richard Nixon, *United States Foreign Policy in the 1970's*, A report to the Congress, February 18, 1970, p. 19.
2   Robert Semple, Jr., 'Nixon to Revive Council's Power,' *New York Times*, January 1, 1969, pp. 1–10.
3   Quoted in *ibid*.
4   Peter Grose, 'Kissinger Gains a Key Authority in Foreign Policy,' *New York Times*, February 5, 1969, pp. 1, 8.

5 John P. Leacacos, 'Kissinger's Apparat,' *Foreign Policy*, Winter 1971–72, p. 7.

6 Quoted in William Beecher, 'New Panel to Coordinate Defence Outlay and Policy,' *New York Times*, November 29, 1969, p. 16.

7 John P. Leacacos, op. cit., pp. 7–8. The 'Forty Committee' authorised a CIA fund of $400,000 at its June 1970 meeting to discuss the Chilean situation, to be used to support anti-Allende media operations. However, Colby refused to divulge the extent to which CIA operations in Chile were authorised by the 'Forty Committee':

> 'We have had . . . various relationships over the years in Chile with various groups. In some cases this was approved by the National Security Council and it has meant some assistance to them.' Quoted in Tad Szulc, 'The View from Langley,' *Washington Post*, October 21, 1973, p. C5.

8 *Ibid.* Also see comments of U. Alexis Johnson, Under-Secretary of State for Political Affairs, on the operation of the National Security Council in U.S. Congress, House, Committee on Foreign Affairs, Subcommittee on National Security Council and Scientific Developments, *National Security Policy and the Changing World Power Alignments*, 92nd Congress, 2nd Session, May 24, 31; June 7, 14, 21, 28; August 8, 1972. Washington: U.S. Government Printing Office, 1972, p. 375.

9 See 'Nixon Reorganises Intelligence Work,' *New York Times*, November 6, 1971, p. 14; Benjamin Welles, 'Helms Told to Cut Global Expenses," *New York Times*, November 7, 1971, p. 5.

10 *Interview No. 2–16*: Washington, D.C., August 9, 1973.

11 See Popular Unity programme, as printed in North American Congress on Latin America, *New Chile*, 1972, p. 130.

12 Senator Edward M. Kennedy, *Address to the Chicago Council on Foreign Relations*, October 12, 1971, pp. 2–3.

13 Richard Nixon, *U.S. Foreign Policy for the 1970's*, A report to the Congress, February 25, 1971, pp. 53–54. Allende, in reply, noted that 'the interests of the United States and the interests of Latin America fundamentally have nothing in common.' Nonetheless, he emphasised that Chile 'wants to maintain cordial and co-operative relations with all nations in the world and most particularly with the United States. . . .' See Salvador Allende, *Chile's Road to Socialism*, Baltimore: Penguin Books, 1973, pp. 105, 106.

14 Jacob K. Javits, 'OPIC, New Hope for U.S. Participation in the Second Development Decade,' *Address to the International Management Division of the American Management Association*, New York, February 1, 1971, pp. 3–4.

15 *Interview No. 2–16*: Washington, D.C., August 9, 1973.

16 Quoted from a memorandum prepared by Ronald R. Raddatz of the Bank of America, which summarised the initial meeting of the Ad Hoc Committee in January 1971. Representatives of the Bank of America, Anaconda, Kennecott, W. R. Grace Co., Pfizer Chemical, and Ralston Purina attended the meeting. See U.S. Congress, Senate, *Multinational Corporations and United States Foreign Policy, Part 1*, op. cit., p. 44.

17 U.S. Congress, Senate, *Multinational Corporations and United States Foreign Policy, Part 2*, op. cit., pp. 1009–1010, and *Part 1*, op. cit., p. 44.

18 *Ibid.*

19 *Ibid.*, pp. 46–47. By mid-January 1971, ITT officials had visited, or had appointments with, U.S. government officials in the Departments of State, Treasury and Commerce, the National Security Council, the Office of Emergency Preparedness, as well as with Congressional personnel. See *ibid., Part 2*, p. 1052.

20 'An Economic Team from Chile Puts its Case in Washington for Continued Investment by Foreigners,' *New York Times*, February 25, 1971, p. 11.

21 Juan de Onis, 'U.S. Cancellation of Visit by Enterprise Stirs Chile,' *New York Times*, March 7, 1971, p. 3. According to a subsequent report, President Nixon overruled the Pentagon and some senior State Department officials in cancelling the visit. See Benjamin Welles, '4 U.S. Officers to go to Chilean Fete,' *New York Times*, March 18, 1971, p. 3. Throughout this early period, Allende's response to U.S. policy was moderate and restrained. He continued to reiterate Chile's desire to maintain friendly relations with the U.S., and stressed that Chile would 'never provide a military base that might be used against the United States . . .' Quoted in *Facts on File*, April 1–7, 1971, p. 257.

CHAPTER IV

The Brazilian and Peruvian Alternatives

In contrast to the generally hostile response which the election of Allende evoked in U.S. policy-makers, Washington has been exuberant over the behaviour and performance of the Brazilian dictatorship : financial resources have been lavished almost without limit or concern. The existence of a pro-U.S. government in Brazil willing to open its markets, resources and labour to U.S. economic interests and to support U.S. political initiatives was sufficient reason for large, long-term U.S. government financial subsidies to promote U.S. business activity in Brazil. Two basic premises underlie U.S. policy toward Brazil : (1) a country the size of a sub-continent with strong affinity for U.S. capital and dependent on external financing could be a useful strategic ally in maintaining U.S. influence in Latin America or at the very least maintaining the area within the 'free market' zone; (2) the political conditions and dimensions of the Brazilian economy and population were such that a meaningful effort could be mounted by the multi-nationals to promote rapid capital accumulation and expansion based on intensified exploitation of the working-class. No other country in Latin America offered the 'package' of opportunities available in Brazil—and (with the exception of Argentina) none seems capable of providing it. Taking the short view the U.S. pursued a policy of promoting its major ally (Brazil) and neutralising a possible adversary (Peru) as the best way to contain Chile. In other words the political conjuncture in Latin America at the time of the election of Allende offered opportunities to pursue a relentless policy of encirclement but only when this perspective was tempered by a realistic assessment of the limits imposed by different non-socialist development efforts emerging in the region.

Since 1964, the U.S. government has provided over $2 billion in economic and military assistance to the right-wing military dictatorship in Brazil in support of a political environment conducive to U.S. economic penetration. The thrust of U.S. policy is sharply delineated in the following exchange between the Director of U.S. AID in Brazil and the chairman of the Senate subcommittee on Western Hemisphere Affairs during Congressional hearings in 1971:

> *Senator Church.* 'How does the present government, in which we have invested $2 billion, serve the national interests of the United States, in your judgement?'
>
> *Mr (William A.) Ellis.* 'Well, first of all, perhaps I should state what I think some of the U.S. national interests are in Brazil. One of them is the existence of a government or society which is generally consistent with our national, specific national, security interests in the hemisphere, which would not pose a security threat to us. Second would be the protection and expansion, if possible, of our economic interests, trade and investment, in the hemisphere.'
>
> *Senator Church.* 'Can you tell me how large the American private investment is in Brazil today?'
>
> *Mr Ellis.* 'It is somewhat over $1.6 billion.'
>
> *Senator Church.* 'So we have pumped in $2 billion since 1964 to protect a favourable climate of investment that amounts to about $1.6 billion.'
>
> *Mr Ellis.* 'That is only one of the objectives, Mr Chairman.'
>
> *Senator Church.* 'I want to get these things in relation. We have spent $2 billion on a programme one objective of which is the protection of a favourable investment climate for private business interests in this country.'
>
> *Mr Ellis.* 'Yes.'[1]

U.S. direct and indirect external assistance is even more strikingly revealed if we consider the period 1969–1972, when total external assistance authorised to Brazil from all sources was in excess of $2 billion. These sources included the World Bank ($877.3 million), the Inter-American Development Bank ($592 million), the Export-Import Bank ($458.4 million), the International Finance Corporation ($56.3 million), and various United Nations organisations ($20.1 million).[2] U.S. support of over $1 billion in multilateral assistance to Brazil during this three-year period stands in sharp contrast to its policy regarding multilateral aid for Peru and Chile.

U.S. policy toward Brazil has been premised on two basic interrelated themes. First, satisfactory relations with Brazil have been viewed as essential to the overall long-term policy goals of the U.S. in Latin America :

'Certainly a definite desire on the part of Nixon and the administration to maintain good relations with Brazil. Essentially a geopolitical view. You simply could not allow relations with a country the size and significance of Brazil to deteriorate badly and expect to have a constructive relationship with Latin America. Specific issues caused problems, for example, the fisheries problem and coffee. But these were worked out in a practical sense so that major conflicts were avoided. . . . In retrospect, the will to resolve differences with Brazil was so strong at the highest levels on both sides, that they were resolved to at least avoid confrontations over fisheries and coffee issues.'[3]

Secondly, U.S. policy-makers have responded favourably to the Brazilian development strategy, based on foreign multinational corporate investment, political repression of the lower classes, the reconcentration of wealth in the hands of the upper class and a developing consumer-oriented middle class. Assistant Secretary of State for Inter-American Affairs Charles Meyer summed up the U.S. attitude : 'We consider that Brazil is a country whose development record has been—well, it is statistical (sic), the development record has been transcendental.'[4] Some policy-makers have attempted to rationalise the repressive aspects of the development process by reference to national character explanations. 'No-one condones the repression. The problem is that Brazilian authorities have always acted brutally toward the people. That is, there is no political newness to the idea of beating someone with a club. Unfortunately, an old Brazilian habit.'[5]

A more commonplace response has been, on the one hand, to minimise the extent of the repression and, on the other, to focus on its positive aspects, viz., its contribution to the creation of political control of the lower class and a suitable climate for foreign investment and profit maximisation. This view is discussed in detail by a State Department official whose involvement with post-1964 U.S. policy toward Brazil has been considerable :

'If you are talking about censorship and the loss of complete political freedom, torture of prisoners, this does go on to some extent. Much of the censorship is self-administered. A good bit of tolerance in it. Not our way, but in a way legitimate. Don't want energies/efforts of the country diverted. I don't feel that development is taking place by oppressing any people and sweating it out of the people by having them tighten their belts. Development is taking place applying classical economics, with sensitivity to good communication between government and business sectors and agricultural sectors. Feeling is that economic growth is clearly the overall objective of the country. They are doing it with good economic policies, they stimulate investment, they let investment be rewarded, exceptional profit opportunities.

'Most Brazilians are apathetic to censorship and torture. They are pretty satisfied with the way things are going. They have provided a certain amount of stability in the political/social situation. Don't see parades broken up on the streets, don't have riots, terrorist groups broken up, greater feeling of calm.'[6]

Nor could the impact of the socialist government in Chile be discounted in any discussion of the evolution of U.S. policy towards Brazil in the early 1970's. A senior U.S. policy adviser on Latin America, while dismissing any 'explicit' attempt to build up Brazil as a counterweight to Chile within the hemisphere, agreed, however, that this consideration was 'certainly a factor' in the minds of policy-makers. '(They) considered Brazil in the context of Latin America and a Marxist Chile.'[7]

During the period 1969 to 1971, U.S. policy-makers adopted a position of hostility towards the governing military junta in Peru, over the latter's seizure or expropriation of properties belonging to such U.S. multinational corporations as Standard Oil of New Jersey, W. R. Grace Company, and Gulf Oil Corporation. A top U.S. policy-maker explained the relationship between business and U.S. policy in the following manner :

'The United States Government has declared a responsibility to protect the legitimate interests of American investors overseas . . . In the particular case of Peru the United States policy is one of reasonableness. We seek and indeed insist that the Government of Peru give prompt, adequate, and effective compensation for the properties and assests which it has, in the exercise of its sovereign power, taken.'[8]

In effect the U.S. government was assuming the right to determine

Peru's development priorities arguing that scarce foreign exchange earnings be diverted away from development projects towards paying U.S. corporations.

U.S. bilateral aid to Peru was reduced and U.S. influence within the international financial institutions was successful in drastically affecting the flow of multilateral economic assistance to the military government. Treasury Under-Secretary Walker admitted that a relationship existed between the cutting off of Inter-American Development Bank funds for approximately two years and the expropriation (without compensation) of International Petroleum Company in 1968.[9]

Nonetheless, the overall U.S. response reflected a certain degree of ambivalence regarding Peru's economic nationalism. A former high-ranking U.S. policy adviser on Latin America within the National Security Council recalled the divergent interdepartmental positions :

'My feeling was that Peru represented a significant, perhaps even a positive, evolution in Latin America and one we could work with if we could not allow IPC to override the entire relationship . . . On the whole, the relationship was better than it might have been if certain interest groups and elements had been predominant within the structure of the U.S. government, that is, people who pushed sanctions and the hard line. The hard-liners were primarily State Department lawyers, the Defence Department. . . . The NSC staff tended to be softer-lined on Peru. We argued for, and continued to push for, avoiding allowing the economic issues to override the larger political relationship. Some in the State Department also favoured that. The Secretary of State tended to be harder-lined than some of his staff people.'[10]

Unlike the case of Chile, expropriations in Peru were not intended to result in a socialist transformation but to modify Peru's terms of dependency and to provide a basis for industrialisation with the inclusion of foreign capital. Dominant policy-makers distinguished between changes *within* capitalist property relations in Peru (the shift from a laissez-faire agro-mineral export society dependent on the U.S. to a statist industrialising society with a variety of sources of external finance—'diversified' dependency) and changes *away* from capitalism in Chile. This important *political* distinction was the basis for making the issue of nationalisation of U.S. property in one instance negotiable and in the other a point of confrontation.

Beginning in late 1971, a visible change in U.S. policy to Peru began to take shape. The decision was the result of the convergence of a number of factors: 'the proven durability and stability'[11] of the military government; its domestic anti-communism, and a development strategy of capitalist modernisation-from-above combined with restricted mass mobilisation from below; compensation settlements with W. R. Grace and Gulf Oil and only limited restrictions on profit remittances abroad; continuing negotiations on the IPC issue; and, in general, what one State Department official called 'a reassessment (by Peru) of the role of foreign investment.'[12] Economically, the Peruvian military government continued to control and limit the role of foreign capital within a mixed economy. However, these constraints and further nationalisations were accompanied by new concessions to foreign capital. Major U.S. and foreign oil companies signed a number of new exploration contracts with the junta, and increasing foreign participation was evidenced in new industrial and mining undertakings. Peruvian economic nationalism was concerned to redefine, not eliminate, dependence on foreign investment.

A further consideration in the thinking of U.S. policy-makers was the emergence of a socialist government in Chile. One former U.S. Ambassador to Latin America characterised the 'new flexibility' toward Peru as part of a policy designed to isolate Chile from the rest of the hemisphere.[13] Another senior policy-maker suggested that this strategy was an important factor in U.S. government deliberations: 'We clearly saw from the beginning a distinction between Peru and Chile, [this is] how we felt about events then affecting our interests.'[14]

Indicative of this changing policy was an increasing tendency to separate specific conflicts involving U.S. investor interests and to support the view 'that Peru had a significance larger and more important than the (particular) investment dispute.'[15] Under-Secretary of State for Security Assistance Curtis W. Tarr elaborated on this shift in emphasis:

'We have disagreements, obviously, with respect to fishing rights, but this does not mean that across-the-board, we disagree with the Peruvians. It does not mean that our relationships on that one point alone are absolutely sour. The American contacts with Peru are considerably more extensive than those that are affected, either by their seizure of plants or by the seizure of our fishing boats. At a time when Peru was actually seizing some of our corporate assets, there were other American corporations who were investing in Peru.'[16]

In June 1973, U.S. Secretary of State William Rogers made an official visit to Peru and declared the U.S. government's support for the military junta's 'constructive nationalism,' even though compensation for expropriated U.S. properties (IPC and W. R. Grace) remained outstanding.[17] Within the hemispheric and international financial agencies, the U.S. government moved to support multilateral loans and credits to Peru. In August and September 1973 it voted in favour of two Inter-American Development Bank loans to Peru totalling $35.6 million and one World Bank loan. The U.S. Executive Director in the World Bank described Peru's attitude towards outstanding investment disputes as 'reasonable' in supporting the $25 million loan for agricultural development.[18]

These actions coincided with a U.S. decision to resume negotiations with Peru in an attempt to resolve a series of disputes involving U.S.-owned properties which had been nationalised without compensation. James R. Greene, senior vice-president of Manufacturers Hanover Trust Co., was designated by President Nixon to act as his personal representative to the Peruvian government. The subsequent nationalisation of a subsidiary of the U.S. Cerro Corporation did not affect the status of these negotiations because of a Peruvian willingness to discuss the question of compensation.[19] The agreement that emerged had both short-term and long-term consequences. It accommodated the immediate Peruvian position, while increasing the country's long-term indebtedness to the United States. In essence, the U.S., through the First National Bank of Boston, has agreed to extend $150 million in loans to Peru, $74 million of which is to be paid directly to five nationalised U.S. companies (Cerro Corporation, W. R. Grace & Co., the Starkist Foods subsidiary of the H. J. Heinz Company, Goldkist Inc., and Cargill Inc.). Conspicuously missing from this list was International Petroleum Company. The other $76 million will be paid to the U.S. government for distribution to other U.S. companies whose assets were nationalised by the Peruvian military government.[20] This willingness 'to settle outstanding problems with the United

States' was an important factor in the decision of the World Bank consultative group on Peru to commit over $1.9 billion in external financing over a three-year period beginning in early 1974.[21]

'U.S. policy toward Peru,' observed a U.S. policy adviser, 'has developed surprisingly well. The one contentious issue is IPC. But other than that, there seems to be a disposition on the part of the Peruvians to take an amicable posture toward the U.S. on some issues. There is no overt hostility. In the United States, there is a feeling that the Peruvian model is certainly preferable to the Chilean model.'[22]

The emergence of a socialist government in Chile had a significant impact on U.S policies toward Peru and Brazil :

> 'Chile helped make it possible to keep open the relationship with Peru and to avoid the problems with Brazil. The concern over Chile governed by a Marxist government led people within the U.S. government to feel that it was more important than they realised to maintain constructive relations with the Latin American countries.'[23]

Conclusion

The existence of democratic-socialist Chile forced the U.S. to come to terms with Peruvian nationalism. The U.S. preferred to accept limited nationalisations that contributed to stabilising a régime supporting a mixed economy than to risk radicalising the situation in Peru through confrontation tactics. Beginning in early 1971 the U.S. realised that the nationalist measures in Chile could strengthen political forces in Peru which were pressuring for a more rapid and thorough transformation. To continue its intransigent policy of economic pressure without any substantial access points in the régime (in contrast to Chile) would provide the Peruvians with no option but to take measures following the Chilean pattern.

Brazil and Peru appeared to represent alternative capitalist development models to the Chilean. In Brazil it appears that the emphasis is on promoting foreign investment to stimulate industrialisation while in Peru the emphasis appears to be on state capital. However a closer examination would reveal that Peruvian development is more comparable to an *earlier* period of Brazilian development during which the State undertook to promote a series of investment projects in heavy industry, infrastructure and natural resources development. It could be the case that Peruvian statism is merely laying the groundwork for a later period in which the door will be opened for large-scale foreign investment. Certainly the decisions taken by the junta do not preclude that future option. And it appears that U.S. policy is premised on that possibility—leaving aside the investment possibilities that exist even today. In any case, during the late 1960's and early 1970's U.S. policy-makers were greatly influenced by what they described as the successful economic growth pattern in Brazil. The capacity of the régime to hold down wages and effectively to exclude nationalist and trade union activities facilitated the process of private accumulation and capital expansion by the multi-national corporations. While the Brazilian experience presented itself to U.S. policy-makers as a model for Latin America, Brazil served as an active base of political support of U.S. policies in Chile.[24] Hence while U.S. policy was directed at 'containing' Peruvian nationalism within the boundaries of a mixed economy and limiting Peru's political ties with Chile, in Brazil the U.S. sought to promote Brazilian expansionism and to increase its ties with Chile. . . . with the opposition groups and military officials. Hence the U.S. concern with Chile caused it to accommodate to Peruvian nationalism and to expand its commitments and ties with Brazil. Hence while the U.S. sought to influence events in Chile, it was influenced by experiences in Brazil: the logic of these political developments was the effort to transplant to Chile the experience in Brazil.

NOTES

1 U.S. Congress, Senate, Committee on Foreign Relations, Subcommittee on Western Hemisphere Affairs, *United States Policies and Programmes in Brazil*, 92nd Congress, 1st Session, May 4, 5, and 11, 1971. Washington: U.S. Government Printing Office, 1971, pp. 165–166. Also see U.S. Congress, House, Subcommittee of the Committee on Government Operations, *U.S. Aid Operations in Latin America under the Alliance for Progress*, 90th Congress, 2nd Session, January 24, 25, 27, 29; February 1, 2, 4, 6, 8, 9, 12, 13, and 15, 1969. Washington: U.S. Government Printing Office, 1969, pp. 431–780.

2   U.S. General Accounting Office, Report to the Congress, *U.S. Foreign Aid to Education*: *Does Brazil Need it?* No. B133283, July 30, 1973, Washington, D.C., p. 17. This study criticised U.S. aid to the Brazilian education system for 'directly and indirectly' reinforcing the prevailing distortions within the system. 'Our review showed that U.S. education assistance efforts were not designed to improve the inequities in the Brazilian system including inequitable distribution of education opportunities between urban and rural areas and disparity in education spending between the affluent and poor areas.' (pp. 34, 40).

3   *Interview No. 2–16*: Washington, D.C., August 9, 1973. In an analysis of the fishing agreement signed between the U.S. and Brazil in September 1972, Senator Clayborne Pell perceptively observed that the 'compact without addressing the controversial sovereignty question, is primarily designed to forestall any confrontation before the 1973 International Law of the Sea Conference. Its provisions completely avoid the disputed issue concerning Brazil's 200-mile territorial sea and are written solely in terms of conservation.' See Senator Pell, *Agreement with Brazil concerning Shrimp*, Senate, 92nd Congress, 2nd Session, Executive Rept. 92–37, October 2, 1972, p. 2; U.S. Congress, Senate, Committee on Foreign Relations, Subcommittee on Oceans and International Environment, *Shrimp Agreement with Brazil*, 92nd Congress, 2nd Session, September 28, 1972. Washington: U.S. Government Printing Office, 1972.

4   U.S. Congress, House, Committee on Foreign Affairs, Subcommittee on Inter-American Affairs, *New Directions for the 1970's – Part 2: Development Assistance Options for Latin America*, 92nd Congress, 1st Session, February 18, July 12, 19, 26, 27 and August 4, 1971. Washington: U.S. Government Printing Office, 1971, p. 265. Regarding the overall relationship, a State Department official responded similarly: 'I would think that we are, right now, at a high point of relations between the U.S. and Brazil. At a high plateau of excellent relations that I don't believe it is possible to get any better.' *Interview No. 2–1*: U.S. Department of State, June 19, 1973.

5   *Interview No. 2–3*: U.S. Department of State, June 11, 1973.

6   *Interview No 2–1*: U.S. Department of State, June 19, 1973.

7   *Interview No. 2–16*: Washington, D.C., August 9, 1973

8   Statement of Charles A. Mayer, Assistant Secretary of State for Inter-American Affairs. U.S. Congress, Senate, Committee on Foreign Relations, Subcommittee on Western Hemisphere Affairs, *United States Relations with Peru*, 91st Congress, 1st Session, April 14, 16 and 17, 1969. Washington: U.S. Government Printing Office, 1969, p. 117.

9   See U.S. Congress, House, Committee on Banking and Currency, Subcommittee on International Finance, *To Authorise the United States to Provide Additional Financial Resources to the Asian Development Bank and the Inter-American Development Bank*, 92nd Congress, 1st Session, October 26, 1971. Washington: U.S. Government Printing Office, 1971, p. 139. See also Murray Rossant, 'The Big Stick is Now Economic,' *New York Times*, October 10, 1971, p. E8.

10   *Interview No. 2–16*: Washington, D.C., August 9, 1973.

11   Richard W. Dye, 'Peru, the United States, and Hemisphere Relations,' *Inter-American Economic Affairs*, Autumn 1972, p. 73.

12   Quoted in Mark L. Chadwin, 'Foreign Policy Report: Nixon Adminis-

tration Debates New Position Paper on Latin America,' *National Journal*, January 15, 1972, p. 103.

13 *Ibid.*

14 *Interview No. 2–21*: U.S. Department of State, August 21, 1973.

15 *Interview No. 2–16*: Washington, D.C., August 9, 1973.

16 U.S. Congress, House, Committee on Appropriations, Subcommittee on Foreign Operations and Related Agencies, *Foreign Assistance and Related Agencies Appropriations for 1974, Part 1*, 93rd Congress, 1st Session. Washington: U.S. Government Printing Office, 1973, p. 1116.

17 Quoted in 'Secretary Rogers' Latin American Tour Brings No Concrete Changes in Policy,' *Business Latin America*, June 7, 1973, p. 179. 'We don't oppose foreign investment,' declared Peruvian foreign minister, Miguel de la Flor, in commenting on the oil contracts awarded to U.S. companies. 'We want it and we need it. But we don't want it to occur the way it did prior to 1968, when it led to Peru's political and economic dependency.' Quoted in John P. Wallach, 'Dispute Over Copper Mines Perils U.S.-Peru Relations,' *Washington Post*, August 16, 1973, p. G13.

18 See 'Secretary Rogers' Latin American Tour Brings No Concrete Changes in Policy,' op. cit., p. 179; Lewis H. Diuguid, 'U.S. Relaxes Policy on Loans to Peru,' *Washington Post*, September 20, 1973, p. A21; 'Peru: High Stakes,' *Latin America*, September 14, 1973, p. 295; International Bank for Reconstruction and Development, *Bank Press Release*, No. 73/63, August 17, 1973; U.S. Congress, House, Committee on Banking and Currency, Subcommittee on International Finance, *Providing for Additional U.S. Contributions to the Asian Development Bank and the International Development Association*, 93rd Congress, 1st Session, November 14; December 3 and 6, 1973. Washington: U.S. Government Printing Office, 1973, p. 17.

19 See 'Cerro Unit Nationalised by Peru: Compensation Talks are Progressing,' *Wall Street Journal*, January 2, 1974, p. 4. On the Greene appointment, see Richard Lawrence, 'World Bank Approves Loan to Peru,' *Journal of Commerce*, August 15, 1973, p. 1. Manufacturers Hanover, at the time, was in the process of preparing to lead a consortium of U.S. banks in lending Peru $130 million in credits. See 'Peru: High Stakes,' op cit., p. 295. The willingness of U.S. private banks to re-open the lines of credit to Peru was first evidenced in April, when Wells Fargo Bank of California made arrangements for a $130 million loan to the military government. A U.S. banker resident in Peru at the time explained the decision to invest: 'Frankly, we feel Peru is a very good risk. . . . This is a stable government— whether it's left leaning or not. There are no riots in the streets, and there is a relatively strong currency.' Quoted in Jonathan Kandell, 'U.S. Aid Embargo Straining Peru Ties,' *New York Times*, April 18, 1973, p. 8.

20 Stephen Morrow, 'U.S., Peru Agreement Seen Near,' *Washington Post*, February 8, 1974, p. A17; H. J. Maidenberg, 'Peru Will Pay $76 Million For Seized U.S. Concerns,' *New York Times*, February 20, 1974, p. 4; 'U.S. Settles Feud on Eleven Firms Peru Nationalised,' *Wall Street Journal*, February 20, 1974, p. 4.

21 Stephen Klaidman, 'Peru-U.S. Scars are Healing,' *Washington Post*, December 26, 1973, p. A16.

22 *Interview No. 2–18*: National Security Council, August 14, 1973.

23 *Interview No. 2–16*: Washington, D.C., August 9, 1973.
24 The 1964 Brazilian military coup was an important point of support
    for the Chilean right and other opponents of the Allende government.
    Brazilian business and private groups who played critical roles in the
    overthrow of the Goulart government in 1964 were, in fact, actively
    involved in channelling thousands of dollars and considerable quantities
    of arms to anti-Allende organisations in Chile as well as in the training
    of Chilean rightists in the politics of coup-making. The Brazilians were
    instrumental in getting the Chilean right and the Christian Democratic
    Party to set up political 'think tanks' to coordinate anti-government
    strategy (a successful tactic in the Brazilian case). The Brazilians also
    pointed out to their Chilean counterparts that the manipulation of
    women in support of the coup strategy was essential: 'We ourselves
    created a large and successful women's movement, the Campaign for
    Women, and Chile copied it.' It was a crucial factor, the Brazilians
    emphasised, in giving the military the impression 'that they have wide
    civilian support.' For a detailed analysis of the Brazilian involvement,
    see Marlisle Simons, 'The Brazilian Connection,' *Washington Post*,
    January 6, 1974, p. B3.

CHAPTER V

U.S. Foreign Economic Policy and the Blockade of Chile

The existence of alternative capitalist development poles to the Chilean strengthened U.S. efforts to thwart its socialist experiment. In addition, however, there were two other basic considerations which have to be taken into account in analysing U.S. policy. The growth of economic competition from Western and Eastern Europe, Japan, China and the U.S.S.R. offered Latin American countries the possibility (over the medium run) of diversifying their sources of external finance and subsequently weakening their economic ties and dependence on the U.S. and the latter's political influence in the area. The second consideration pertained to the countries within the region, what was described by numerous influential officials variously as the ripple/domino effect : a successful effort by Chile would encourage economic nationalists elsewhere. Conversely if the Chilean experience could be induced to fail, the U.S. and its apologists could write and argue about the 'failures' of socialism. Under conditions of growing competition, in which it appears the U.S. was losing ground, U.S. policy-makers may have felt that their hegemonic position in the region could no longer be maintained by strictly economic relations, but that there was a need to promote strict and direct political control through a dependent military régime. The efforts to bolster the sagging fortunes of U.S. economic interests in the face of external competition and internal threats resulted in the establishment of the Council on International Economic Policy, an organisation which fitted in nicely with President Nixon's desire for a rational and coherent foreign policy approach based on long-term structural developments.

The U.S. government's negative response to the election of Allende in September 1970—rooted in a conflict of political and

economic interests—crystallised into specific policies shortly thereafter. The White House and the National Security Council settled
on an overall strategy of 'controlled escalation' of hostile measures
in which periods of conflict would alternate with periods of negotiation. This strategy involved the combining of a two-pronged
attack : prolonged economic confrontation and the gradual disaggregation of the Chilean state. The tactics designed to realise
economic dislocation in Chile were essentially threefold : an
international credit squeeze, via mobilisation of support for the
U.S. position within the international financial institutions and
amongst Chile's international creditors; the elaboration of an
ideology of 'lack of creditworthiness' based on conditions (inflation,
disinvestment, etc.) created, in large part, by the U.S. credit blockade; and the identification of gradual economic deterioration with
internal government policy, thus creating the economic basis for
polarising Chilean society in a manner favourable to the large
propertied groups. These efforts were parallelled by the deepening
of ties between the U.S. and critical sectors of the Chilean state
(military, police) and private institutions (employer associations).
In the process, these groups were separated from the executive
branch and its national project and mobilised in support of U.S.
policy goals. The U.S. government's strategy of a gradual accumulation of internal forces stood in opposition to the initial more
narrowly conceived responses of certain U.S. corporations (ITT,
etc.) with major economic investments in Chile. As one official in
the National Security Council told us :

> 'A major consideration, both in general expropriation policy
> and in the case of Chile, was that it is all very well to go in and
> support one company, but the costs involved in going into Chile
> would be very high. . . . no country should sacrifice its overall
> relations or interests or other groups in the country for the sake of
> one interest group.'[1]

U.S. policy-makers continued to cloak their policies in the
rhetoric of moderation and compromise and to express public
interest in negotiations with the Allende government aimed at
resolving outstanding differences. However a high CIA official
noted a different aspect of the negotiating posture '. . . our intelligence requirements, in the (debt) negotiations between the United
States and Chile, would be to try and find out, through our sources,

what their reactions to a negotiating session were, what their reading of our position was, what their assessment of the state of negotiations is.'[2] U.S. policy-makers claimed 'a real effort to avoid a direct confrontation,' 'an unwavering willingness on our part to take the extra step,' 'continuous negotiating,' and 'keep(ing) the door open.'[3] In point of fact, however, this professed desire for negotiations was but a tactical element in the overall U.S. strategy. It was designed to allow time for the economic squeeze gradually to engender a general societal deterioration, and direct military intervention in the political arena. In a secret memorandum to the State Department in early 1971, U.S. Ambassador Nathaniel Davis emphasised that a military coup would only occur when public opposition to the Allende government became 'so overwhelming, and discontent so great, that military intervention is overwhelmingly invited.'[4]

The National Security Council, while maintaining overall responsibility for policy toward Chile ('Chile's an NSC matter,' said one U.S. official[5]) delegated the application of specific measures to the appropriate government agencies. This delegation of authority allowed NSC officials to mediate between different agencies and departments over the specific measures adopted to implement policy. The NSC sought to maximise pressure in Chile but without forcing a 'premature' rupture in relations (i.e., before a coup could be consummated). One NSC official described the tactical infighting and their own role in the following terms :

'NSC input has generally been on the side of counselling a more moderate approach to dealing with these countries. This puts us in the middle of a number of fires. The Treasury take a hard line on expropriations and the President takes a hard line too. The State Department takes a very cautious line— traditional—in dealing with these problems. The NSC point of view leans toward the State point of view. . . .

'Treasury was very hard-line, and had a strong input, but their views were not dissimilar from those of the President because Connally and the President talked a lot. The State Department line was more moderate, although it would have condoned nothing. The NSC was pretty much in the middle. Our general feeling was 'let's keep the door open'. The position followed came out quite similar to the NSC position.'[6]

These inter-departmental differences of opinion were primarily different appreciations and estimates of the most effective mix between external coercion and internal pressure as means of realising the desired changes in Chile and Latin America.

In January 1971, at the suggestion of NSC adviser Henry Kissinger, President Nixon established a Council on International Economic Policy (CIEP) to 'provide a clear, top-level focus on international economic issues and achieve consistency between international and domestic economic policy.'[7] It represented a decision on the part of the U.S. government that 'economic interests cut directly across foreign policy considerations and thus bear on military and diplomatic commitments abroad.'[8] One of the purposes envisaged in establishing the Council was 'protecting and improving the earnings of foreign investments.'[9] The newly appointed Director of CIEP, Peter Peterson, outlined the basis of the new foreign economic policy in a study requested by the President :

'The tradition of the Yankee trader, which we may proudly invoke, is a tradition that placed its faith in more trade, not less. And now that others have become first-rate economic powers in their own right, there must also be the realisation that political, economic and security questions are inseparable in long-range policy planning, and that it is the global relationships which in the end must be protected and nurtured. In an increasingly economic, interdependent and competitive era, we shall also find increasingly that economics is politics.'[10]

An NSC staff member was more concise : 'We are willing now to push harder on economic interests . . .'[11] A key policy-maker in the implementation of this new policy was Secretary of the Treasury John Connally, whose 'unparalleled'[12] influence with President Nixon enabled him to reassert Treasury's pre-eminence in the making of foreign policy as it affected international economic policy and vice versa. He utilised his position as chairman of the National Advisory Council on International Monetary and Financial Policies —which is charged with recommending what position the U.S. government should take on loan requests from the international financial institutions—to make Treasury 'slightly more equal than the others on close votes.'[13] Furthermore, the U.S. Executive Directors on the boards of the World Bank, Inter-American

Development Bank, and the International Development Association were Treasury officials, directly answerable to the Secretary of Treasury.

The close convergence of government policy-business interests was made evident in response to a decision by Ecuador to expropriate the property of All American Cables & Radio, a subsidiary of International Telephone and Telegraph (ITT). The Ecuadorian government offered ITT $575,000 in compensation as against the latter's demand for $600,000. The corporation then proceeded to pressure the U.S. government to invoke sanctions and withhold all future economic assistance to Ecuador until the ITT demand had been met. 'ITT was determined to teach the Ecuadorians a lesson as a matter of principle,' one U.S. official observed. 'They were trying to teach all of Latin America a lesson.' These actions were successful, largely because, according to this official, the Treasury Department 'adopted the ITT position uncritically.'[14]

The U.S. government refused to accept new loan applications from Ecuador during most of 1971, and a $15.8 million AID authorisation was held up until a settlement was reached with ITT. In the Inter-American Development Bank, the U.S. was able to forestall approval of three loans to Ecuador totalling $21.5 million until after the conflict had been resolved in favour of ITT. 'According to sources in Washington well informed about U.S. economic policy in South America, the Ecuador case was important because it served notice that the United States would not flinch from invoking sanctions even when a token sum of money was involved. It represented a solid victory for Treasury Department hard-liners.'[15]

Testimony before Congressional committees by high-ranking Treasury officials underlined the decisive role of the Department in the formulation and execution of foreign economic policy. 'Developing countries,' declared Charles E. Walker, Under-Secretary of the Treasury, 'must . . . tread very lightly in using expropriation of foreign investments unless there is evidence that satisfactory progress is being made toward settlement of expropriation disputes.'[16] During the first half of 1971, the U.S. abstained from voting on a World Bank livestock loan for Bolivia over the question of compensation for expropriated U.S. properties :

'. . . despite settlement of the Gulf Oil dispute, other expropriations have taken place and evidence is as yet insufficient to conclude that progress toward compensation is being made. A parallel position was taken on an Inter-American Development Bank loan to Bolivia related to the World Bank loan.'[17]

In June, the U.S. Executive Director to the World Bank, Robert E. Wieczorowiski, abstained from voting on a $6 million loan to Guyana for flood control, contending that it was too early to make a judgement on the 'progress' of compensation negotiations between the Guyanese government and a recently nationalised Canadian bauxite corporation (ALCAN), with substantial U.S. ownership :

Mr Reuss. 'Did the President of the World Bank indicate a position as to whether this proposed loan to Guyana should go forward in that it was accompanied by evidence that progress was being made toward the resolution of the ALCAN expropriations?'
Mr Wieczorowiski. 'There was not what you would call a formal provision of evidence but I think it was clear that in bringing the project forward there was a determination on the Bank's part that this policy was being met.'
Mr Reuss. 'Did you abstain on your own or did the Secretary of the Treasury instruct you to?'
Mr Wieczorowiski. 'My actions within the World Bank group do have the guidance of the Treasury and the NAC (National Advisory Council) and I was acting with such guidance.'
Mr Reuss. 'And their guidance was to tell you to abstain.'
Mr Wieczorowiski. 'Yes, sir.'[18]

The loan was supported by the other twenty members of the World Bank board, including the Canadian representative. One Treasury policy-maker explained the U.S. decision in these words : '. . . when we directed an abstention or negative vote on Guyana, we were concerned that if Guyana followed through on its bauxite nationalisation there would be a wave of nationalisations sweeping the Caribbean. (Nationalisation activities setting a precedent) was our long-run concern, particularly in the Andean nations and in the Caribbean.'[19]

Before the House Subcommittee on Inter-American Affairs, John R. Petty, Assistant Secretary of the Treasury for International Affairs, maintained that the U.S. position on compensation pay-

ments for expropriated U.S.-owned properties was consonant with
long-standing World Bank policy. He questioned 'the policy of the
Bank in lending when there were unresolved expropriatory issues
outstanding.' The U.S. vote with respect to Guyana was 'a signal
to the management of the World Bank that we thought that
administration of the policy wasn't quite the way we read the cards.'
He concluded with an explicit statement of the U.S. position :

> '. . . there is an appropriate place for a policy where the U.S.
> government can support the activities of its nationals abroad
> through a fair and balanced policy of deterrents, indicating that
> there are economic costs involved in expropriation for the host
> country, and that if they seek to pursue their policy, the costs
> will be incurred.'[20]

The U.S. government was opposed, not merely to expropriation
without adequate compensation, but to the very principle of
nationalisation itself.

In an interview with *Business Week*, Secretary of the Treasury
Connally was quoted as saying that 'the U.S. can afford to be
tough with Latin Americans because we have no friends left there
anymore.'[21] The statement was later retracted; its importance lies
not in what it tells us about Latin America (where the U.S. could
count on Brazil, Paraguay, and Central America among others as
'friends'), but about the state of mind of U.S. officials. The wish to
appear 'isolated', the garrison mentality, was a convenient way of
justifying an arbitrary and unilateral policy conceived to support
exclusively narrow U.S. economic interests. Hence U.S. policy of
economic pressure against Allende's Chile was part of a larger
regional policy of general opposition to all efforts at autonomous
national economic development—a policy, as we have seen in the
case of Peru, which was later modified.

U.S. economic pressure on the Allende government, in the form
of declining government, private banking and commercial credits,
began immediately following the 1970 election. U.S. policy was less
a response to specific sector nationalisations than to the more fundamental political and economic issues raised by the fact that a
thorough socialist transformation was envisaged in Chile. The
economic conflicts were the immediate sources of conflict for these
more basic considerations. While keeping this in mind it is important
however to follow the sequence of events that led to confrontation

On September 29, 1971, Allende announced that $774 million would be deducted as excess profits from any compensation due the Anaconda Company and Kennecott Copper Corporation for the nationalisation of their Chilean assets.[22] Since most estimates placed the book value of the nationalised mines at $500 to $600 million, the 'no compensation' decision by the Controler General of Chile was not unexpected.

U.S. policy makers, with increasing support from influential Congressional quarters, reacted angrily to the Chilean actions. They left little doubt that a forthcoming Presidential policy statement would reflect the hardened U.S. position on the treatment of foreign governments who nationalised U.S. investment assets without adequate compensation. A broadside against the Chilean action was soon levelled by influential U.S. officials. 'Obviously in some cases our interests may outweigh the effects of expropriation,' said one U.S. official. 'But generally, countries that expropriate our assets will be on notice that this will generate a fresh policy review at very high levels of government.'[23] Concern was expressed that a 'soft' response to this problem would serve to encourage further expropriations, especially in Africa and Latin America. Robert S. McNamara, president of the World Bank and former U.S. Secretary of Defence, declared his support of the U.S. position in some pointed remarks to the International Centre for Settlement of Investment Disputes. '(He) warned developing countries that a "disquieting" trend by governments to annul agreements with foreign investors could "seriously imperil" their creditworthiness and inhibit investment in their entire region.'[24]

The U.S. Secretary of State, William Rogers, in an official government response, charged Chile with making a 'serious departure from accepted standards of international law' in employing the excess profits concept. In a crude attempt to induce global pressures on Chile, he then threatened to reduce the general level of U.S. aid to the underdeveloped world : '(Chile's) course of action . . . could have an adverse effect on the international development process.'[25] Assistant Secretary of State for Inter-American Affairs Charles Meyer also attacked 'the retroactive application of the "excess profits" concept' and reiterated the U.S. insistence on 'just compensation for expropriated properties.'[26] The excess profits concept was used by U.S. policy-makers to differentiate between Chile and Peru :

'There is a difference of degree between our problems in Chile and our problems in Peru. For example, the Chilean government has enunciated the Allende doctrine which permits them to unilaterally determine whether a given company has made excess profits in the past and deduct those profits from the value of the nationalised property. This is an extreme departure which has a number of implications around the world. . . .

'Peru didn't charge excess profits (and) their criteria is different, and much less difficult in terms of international law, in that they say that the arbitration provisions under which Standard Oil operated there were faulty. This is a lot different from saying "You made too much money and we are going to take it away from you." None of the other cases in Peru are remotely comparable. But at least the principle of compensation is recognised in Peru, with the exception of IPC, as compared to Chile.'[27]

U.S. corporate interests responded in a similar vein. The excess profits statement signified that 'the issue (was) no longer simply between the companies and Chile but between Washington and Santiago.'[28] In October, the executives of six U.S. corporations with holdings in Chile (Anaconda, Ford Motor Company, First National City Bank, Bank of America, Ralston Purina, and ITT) met with Secretary of State Rogers for an 'open discussion' of their predicament and the possible response of their government.[29] Rogers opened the meeting by stating that 'the Nixon Administration was a "business Administration" in favour of business and its mission was to protect business,'[30] and voiced concern that Chile's actions could have a 'domino effect' throughout Latin America in the absence of strong U.S. retaliatory action. He also raised the issue of an informal embargo on spare parts and materials being shipped to Chile and, according to some reports, told the corporation executives that the U.S. government intended to invoke the Hickenlooper Amendment and eliminate all aid to Chile unless the expropriated copper companies received swift and adequate compensation. The Treasury Department, meanwhile, was attempting to formulate a ruling (through the Internal Revenue Service) whereby the copper companies would be granted a $175 million tax deduction on their copper losses in Chile.[31]

During September/October 1971, ITT elaborated in detail on

possible U.S. government policy options in dealing with the Allende government. In a memorandum that proposed the formation of a special NSC task force to put pressure on Chile, the following actions were suggested :

1. Continue loan restrictions in the international banks such as those the Export-Import Bank has already exhibited.
2. Quietly have large U.S. private banks do the same.
3. Confer with foreign banking sources with the same thing in mind.
4. Delay buying (copper) from Chile over the next six months.
5. Bring about a scarcity of U.S. dollars in Chile.
6. Discuss with CIA how it can assist the six-month squeeze.
7. Get to reliable sources within the Chilean Military.[32]

A revised version of the ITT 1970 'White Paper' on Chile discussed possible State Department actions :

1. Exercise the United States veto in the Inter-American Development Bank with respect to several Chile loan applications with the bank.
2. Through use of U.S. veto or pressure, shut off any pending or future World Bank loans to Chile.
3. Continue the refusal of the U.S. Export-Import Bank to grant any loans to Chile.
4. Indicate the State Department's strong displeasure with Chile's flagrant disregard for norms of international law in nationalisation without adequate compensation and urge the U.S. banking community to refrain from extending any further credits to Chile. If possible, extend this to international banking circles.
5. Halt all AID projects that are still in the government pipe lines.
6. Embargo imports from Chile into the United States. (Value of Chile exports to the U.S. now is about $154 million.)
7. Enlist the support of Chile's neighbours, particularly Argentina, Brazil and Peru (and possibly Bolivia with its new rightist government) to protest in international forums about the reported offer of arms credits to Chile by the Soviet Union . . .[33]

Having deleted the more extreme aspects of their earlier proposals, the proposed ITT strategy converged with U.S. government policy and practice.

The political-economic nature of the U.S. credit blockade of Chile between 1970 and 1973 was sharply delineated in an exchange between the Assistant Secretary of the Treasury for International Affairs, John Hennessy, and the chairman of the Senate Subcommittee on Multinational Corporations, Frank Church, during hearings on the efforts of International Telephone and Telegraph to overthrow the Allende government in 1970 and 1971. Questioned on the immediate termination of credits by U.S. government agencies and the multilateral development institutions to the new Chilean government, Hennessy maintained that these decisions were typically made when new governments came into office whose purpose was to induce 'far-reaching new economic programmes' or 'a whole structural approach':

> *Senator Church.* 'I do not mean to belabour the point, but there has been instances where credit is immediately extended to a new government, not only by our own agencies but by the multilateral institutions. I have in mind what happened in Bolivia, when credit was immediately made available. It is not always necessarily the pattern to wait and see what the Government is going to do before giving credit.'
> *Mr Hennessy.* 'The distinction I am making, the difference here is when far reaching new economic programmes, when a whole new structural approach is about to be undertaken, and at the same time statements are being made about their international obligations, that there are going to be expropriations—those types of things raise doubts in the mind of any banker, and I am sure in the case of these banks' management.'[34]

Between 1964 and 1970, over $1 billion in economic assistance flowed into Chile from the U.S. Agency for International Development, the U.S. Export-Import Bank, the World Bank, and the Inter-American Development Bank. During the same period, $200 to $300 million in short-term lines of commercial credit was continuously available to Chile from U.S. private banks. Almost 80 per cent of all short-term credits came from U.S. suppliers and U.S. banks.[35] Throughout the Allende government's tenure, aid disbursements to Chile from U.S. AID, the U.S. Export-Import Bank, the World Bank (IBRD), and the inter-American Development Bank (IDB) were non-existent or negligible, while short-term lines of credit from U.S. private banks declined to around $30 million. The virtual elimination of long-term development loans from AID, IDB, and IBRD, together with increasing demands for the immediate repayment of debt obligations incurred by the Alessandri and Frei governments, constricted the opportunities for long-term development, planning and investment. The decline in short-term credits drastically affected Chile's capacity to import adequate quantities of essential goods for the day-to-day operation of society, and over time affected the standard of living and economic productivity of the country.

In August 1971, the Export-Import Bank informed the Chilean Ambassador in Washington that any further loans or guarantees from that institution would be dependent on a satisfactory resolution of the copper conflict.[36] It also terminated all loan guarantees to U.S. commercial banks and exporters engaged in business activities in Chile, as well as 'disbursements of direct loans that had been previously negotiated by the Frei government. . . .'[37] The withdrawal of the commercial and political risk insurance programme was directly responsible for the erosion of short-term private bank and supplier credits.

The role of the White House, and presumably the NSC, in these actions was apparently decisive in view of the further incident in volving the Export-Import Bank and Chile at this time. Eximbank chairman Henry Kearns announced in June that a pending loan request by Chile to finance the purchase of three U.S. Boeing passenger jets had been denied because of the lack of proper assurances on compensation for the expropriated U.S. copper companies.[38] A Department of Commerce official termed the decision basically political in nature, and minimised the importance of Chile's credit standing as a factor in the outcome. Although the State Department questioned the likely effect of this decision on current negotiations involving other U.S. interests in Chile, and on 'delicate negotiations elsewhere in Latin America, notably Venezuela,'[39] the White House/Treasury position was upheld. State Department officials contended privately that the final decision to refuse the loan 'was made on "the White House level" under the pressure of private American companies.'[40]

The U.S. government also displayed a 'high profile' within the multilateral aid institutions, particularly the Inter-American Development Bank and the World Bank. With the exception of two educational loans totalling $11.6 million to the Austral and Catholic universities—both opposition educational strongholds— IDB awarded no long-term development loans to the Allende government. A $30 million loan application for the construction of a petrochemical complex was shelved after the U.S. Executive Director voiced strong objections to a Bank plan to send a technical mission to Chile to evaluate the request.[41] A similar situation prevailed in the World Bank which did not make a single loan to the Allende government despite the fact that a number of detailed projects were submitted for consideration. In one instance, an appraisal mission to Chile to evaluate a fruit-processing plant project (part of the agrarian reform programme and considered crucial to improve Chile's balance of payments situation) was cancelled at the request of the State Department.[42] Nevertheless, Chile continued to meet its debt service obligations to the Bank. At the 1972 annual meeting of the Board of Governors of the World Bank, the Chilean representative, Alfonso Inostroza, observed that disbursements from loans approved in the pre-Allende period were approximately equal to Chile's payments to the Bank. 'If no fresh credits are granted to us,' he continued, the time will come when Chile's debt service payments to the Bank exceed the sums which it received from it. The paradox would then come to pass of Chile becoming a net exporter of capital to the World Bank, instead of the Bank assisting Chile.'[43]

In October 1971, a Congressional subcommittee inquired of Treasury Under-Secretary Walker as to what the U.S. position within the World Bank or the Inter-American Development Bank would be in response to a loan request from the Allende government :

'I would put it within the context of an expropriation of property in which there has been absolutely no indication up to this time that the compensation will be adequate or timely. On that basis if a loan to Chile were to come up today in the Inter-American Development Bank or the World Bank—the World Bank has a rule and they would not lend to Chile under these circumstances, but the IDB has no such rule—there is no doubt in my mind what Secretary Connally's instructions to Mr Costanzo (U.S. Executive Director) would be . . .'[44]

The role of the International Monetary Fund with regard to

Chile was somewhat more ambiguous. While the IMF, like the World Bank, conditions aid on a country's general economic policies, officials of the institutions 'are more willing than they were in the past to recognise that their short-term exigencies can have adverse effects on long-term policies and that they ought to take these effects into account in the demands they make on countries wanting to use the Fund's resources.'[45] Under the presidency of Pierre-Paul Schweitzer, the IMF has been prepared to admit 'that its economic demands often were politically unacceptable to governments caught in the exigencies of development.'[46] In the case of Chile, the IMF helped prepare the country's debt renegotiation brief and resisted the U.S. position that Chile accept a 'standby' agreement. IMF loans to Chile of $39.5 million and $42.8 million from the export compensation fund in 1971 and 1972 partly reflected the fact that the Fund 'is not a bank but a mechanism to assist member-countries with foreign exchange difficulties; moreover, since the Fund had clear authority to make compensatory loans for this type of foreign exchange shortfall, the United States did not object.'[47] But perhaps, more importantly, the European members of the IMF appear to have a relatively greater impact on its policies vis-a-vis the United States as compared with their leverage within the World Bank. A U.S. attempt to replace Schweitzer as president of the IMF was vigorously, and successfully, opposed by the Latin American and European members of the Fund. Nevertheless, the partial defeat for the U.S. in the International Monetary Fund over the question of Chile needs to be put in perspective. The IMF only provided Chile with loans for very specific and limited purposes. Long-term development assistance credits remained dependent on the acceptance of austerity IMF 'standby' agreements—which would have limited the Allende government's internal economic autonomy and had a negative impact on the standard of living of the working class, the major social basis of support for the government.

The cumulative impact of U.S. economic pressures on the Chilean economy led to a severe economic deterioration by early 1973, and allowed the U.S. to justify a continued credit squeeze on this basis of Chile's supposed lack of creditworthiness—a situation which previous U.S. policy was designed to bring about. During 1971 and 1972, however, (before the effects of the credit squeeze set in) the Allende government's economic policies compared more than favourably with those of the reformist Frei administration. According to a study by the Inter-American Committee on the Alliance for Progress, a major accomplishment of the Allende government was the elimination of economic stagnation and the achievement of 'a more equitable distribution of the benefits of economic growth . . .'[48] After analysing the government's policies through 1972, the study concluded on the following note :

'In 1972, the country's economy is in a situation of almost full utilisation of its productive capacity, following a year marked by high growth levels. Unemployment has been reduced markedly and a broad process of redistribution of income and accelerated agrarian reform has been carried out.'[49]

Nevertheless, the study also issued a warning :

'According to Secretariat estimates, relief in the payment of service of the debt over the next few years will be necessary in order to maintain an adequate growth rate over that period. Furthermore, if the prospects for copper prices do not change, the estimated growth in the volume of exports will not be sufficient for generating resources for balancing the balance of payments current account.'[50]

Chilean attempts to cope with economic problems resulting from U.S. pressures took the form of a non-confrontation strategy based on alternative sources of financing and new trading partners. Although Chile was able to renegotiate $300 million in debts to foreign governments and private creditors and obtain $600 million in credits and loans from socialist bloc countries and Western sources in 1972, many of these loans and credits '(were) tied to specific development projects and (could) be used only gradually.'[51] The situation was also affected by the precipitous decline in Chile's foreign exchange reserves, resulting from the fact that approximately one third of the country's total export earnings in 1970, 1971, and 1972,[52] went to service the foreign debt—at a time of rising import prices, increasing domestic demand, declining world copper prices, no U.S. credits, and the refusal of the U.S. government (Chile's major creditor) to renegotiate Chile's public debt to the U.S. Finally, U.S. suppliers were now demanding 'cash in advance for essential raw materials and parts sales to Chile.'[53] Chile's efforts were ultimately not adequate to the situation : the country could not at one and the same time meet past external obligations, current economic pressures and develop the economy.

In January 1972, President Nixon outlined a stringent U.S. public position on expropriations, which was intended to define the U.S. position on Chile and Latin America. While acknowledging the State Department's concern with U.S. global foreign policy interests, the statement noted the 're-emergence of the Treasury Department as a central and undisguised directing force in international economic policy.'[54] It began by questioning 'the wisdom of any expropriation . . . even when adequate compensation is paid.' and continued :

'. . . when a country expropriates a significant U.S. interest without making reasonable provision for such compensation to U.S. citizens, we will presume that the United States will not extend new bilateral economic benefits to the expropriating country unless and until it is determined that the country is taking reasonable steps to provide adequate compensation or that there are major factors affecting U.S. interests which require continuance of all or part of these benefits.

'On the face of the expropriatory circumstances just described, we will presume that the United States Government will withhold its support from loans under consideration in multilateral development banks.'[55]

This policy statement provided the legal justification for the Treasury Department's activities since 1969 in pursuit of larger U.S. policy goals. 'Before the January 1972 statement was made public,' a Treasury official pointed out, 'Treasury was already following that position. Treasury had already been applying that policy.' He described specific examples :

'The State Department opposed abstaining on the Guyana vote. This was the Treasury position. On Bolivia in 1971, the U.S. abstained. In the Inter-American Development Bank in 1969, the U.S. abstained on Peru. The director said to us that the U.S. abstained to show its displeasure. The policy statement was a kind of clarification put down on paper. That was more or less the Connally influence, hard-line, that in the case of expropriation, the United States would vote no, or would show its displeasure regarding the proposed loan by, at least, abstaining.'[56]

The State Department sought to interpret the new policy directive as a 'compromise' but one in which 'Treasury got the better part of the deal.'[57] Some Treasury officials tended to concur with this view :

'Secretary Connally did play a key role. He had input directly with Kissinger and the President. He had the policy role with respect to the multilateral financial institutions. But he was not having, by any means, the final word. On the other hand, when the battle was going on between Treasury and State, we won on the expropriation statement and got it out and published. On the other hand, the surveillance group to keep an eye on the expropriations and carry through the policy was put under the control of the State Department.'[58]

Presidential assistant and Executive Director of CIEP Peter Peterson stated that the 'hard-line' policy was designed to provide 'investment security' for U.S. investment capital in the underdeveloped world.[59] Sectors of the U.S. business community, however, disputed this contention, viewing the policy as short-sighted and potentially counterproductive. They expressed concern over its possible effect on the entire investment climate in Latin America, and felt that any application of the sanctions policy to a particular country would eliminate the likelihood of compensation for previously expropriated companies there. They also raised the spectre of the U.S. investor being denied complete access to those countries subject to the sanctions :

'For example, to the extent that U.S. bilateral aid and multilateral aid and multilateral assistance is choked off, and other countries including the USSR and Eastern Europe are invited to fill the gap, U.S. suppliers and investors may find themselves needlessly cut off from the market.'[60]

Finally, it was argued that the expropriation threat was essentially limited to one country, Chile, which was no longer a recipient of U.S. economic assistance :

'By strengthening a policy which fits a situation that is the exception rather than the rule, it could be argued that President Nixon is overresponding and perhaps taking an action which in itself does a basic disservice to the investment climate. It tends to make the investment situation throughout Latin America look infinitely worse than it is.'[61]

The criticisms of the corporate interests were based not on a rejection of the principles enunciated by Nixon but on their applicability to Latin America, a Latin America which they perceived as open and receptive to U.S. capital.

The businessmen saw no need to elaborate a general policy statement about Latin America when the issue at hand was the specific problems affecting U.S. relations with one country—Chile. The thrust of the Nixon policy was clearly aimed at increasing the external economic pressures on the socialist government of Chile, in order to exacerbate internal economic disorder and social conflict and to lessen the attractiveness of the Chilean model to its neighbours. U.S. policy-makers perceived Chile as the linchpin in the Latin American struggle to redefine its political and economic relationships with the United States.

A former NSC staff member with responsibility for Latin America commenting on the situation in August 1973, approximately one month before the military coup, admitted that U.S. policy was geared for a major confrontation :

'. . . to adopt a policy where virtually every investment dispute escalated into a government to government dispute was wrong. That is pretty much where we are right now. It would be difficult for us to isolate investment-expropriation issues from political issues . . . I think it is very difficult for Allende to work out a solution which the U.S. government could ever consider a reasonable one.'[62]

In March 1972, following the January policy statement on expropriation, the Nixon administration vigorously supported passage of the Gonzalez amendment by the U.S. Congress. The amendment required the President to instruct the U.S. Executive Directors in the various multilateral aid institutions to vote against loans or the utilisation of funds for any country which (1) nationalised or expropriated U.S.-owned properties; (2) declared invalid existing agreements with U.S. corporations; or (3) applied discriminatory taxes or other operational restrictions effectively resulting in nationalisation or expropriation. Only Presidential determination that an arrangement for satisfactory compensation has been made, or that the dispute has been submitted to the rules of the Convention for the Settlement of Investment Disputes for arbitration, or that 'good faith negotiations are in progress aimed at providing prompt, adequate, and effective compensation under the applicable principles of international law' could prevent implementation of this 'high profile' policy within the international institutions.[63]

In August 1973, a Treasury Department official assessed the results of this active interventionist policy :

'We find that the United States has been rather successful in blocking those loans (to countries that have expropriated U.S. properties). But there is a difference between the Inter-American Development Bank and the World Bank. In the World Bank, the management decides that loans should be brought up to the Board of Directors. But if the management decides not to bring up the loan, then it doesn't come to a vote. In that sense, I don't know how many loans were turned down because the U.S. view announced it would oppose them. But in the Inter-American Development Bank, the management can bring loans to a vote of the Board of Directors and the countries themselves can do the same. But realising that loans would be voted down if they were brought up, they have not been requested to be voted upon by the interested country. In that sense, the policy has been more effective than we believed that it was.'[64]

In an address to the 1973 annual meeting of the World Bank and the International Monetary Fund in Nairobi, Kenya, U.S. Treasury Secretary George Shultz restated the hard-line U.S. position : '. . . we do not find it reasonable that a nation taking confiscatory steps toward investment that it has already accepted from abroad should anticipate official assistance, bilateral or multilateral.'[65] During a subsequent appearance before a U.S. Congressional subcommittee, he emphasised the necessity of taking 'a really firm stand on the question of expropriation' which he described as 'a disease that has been spreading in the world.'[66]

Clearly the U.S. was able to realise its economic blockade of Chile in large part because international financial agencies are still to a large degree influenced by policy decisions in Washington. It is sufficient for a decision to be reached by the U.S. Executive in order that the major lending institutions begin to fashion their policies and lending criteria accordingly. Earlier we noted the close correspondence between U.S. corporate interests and U.S. government policy and the common purposes and strategies pursued. This web of relations is now extended to include the major 'international' financial institutions which strongly influence the international credit rating of a country. The combined and mutually reinforcing efforts of U.S. corporations and government agencies and international banks sharply diminished the marketing, trade, investment and credit opportunities of Chile throughout the world. No single aspect of the problem can be adequately considered in measuring the impact of the 'economic blockade.' Only by examining the continuous process of escalating pressures in *all* their manifestations can we adequately appreciate the full political consequences of the U.S. initiated and directed efforts to overthrow the Allende government. The inter-locking of business, government and international banking that was discussed above suggest that an international power bloc has emerged whose scope of activity includes the world market and which influences a substantial area of the world's trade and credit.

Within the foreign policy machinery the formulation and direction of foreign economic policy was largely in the hands of Treasury, the agency most closely associated with the private corporate world. While there was a consensus among all agencies in their negative evaluation of the social nature of the Allende government, there were substantial differences at different times over the adoption of specific policy measures. The National Security Council served as a sounding board and mediating body for these conflicting views, modifying and adopting them within the overall perspectives.

NOTES

1   *Interview No. 2–18*: National Security Council, August 14, 1973.
2   Quoted in Tad Szulc, op. cit., October 21, 1973, p. C5.
3   Interviews with various U.S. policy-makers.
4   Quoted in Jack Anderson, 'ITT Hope of Ousting Allende Remote,' *Washington Post*, March 28, 1972, p. B11 and 'A Hint Not Taken: Nixon Avoids Allende," *Washington Post*, December 10, 1972, p. C7.
5   *Interview No. 2–20*: Council on International Economic Policy, August 20, 1973.

6 *Interview No. 2–18*: National Security Council, August 14, 1973.
7 Quoted in Dom Bonafede, 'White House Report: Peterson Unit Helps Shape Tough International Economic Policy,' *National Journal*, October 13, 1971, p. 2241.
8 *Ibid.*, p. 2238.
9 U.S. Congress, House, Committee on Banking and Currency, Subcommittee on International Trade, *To Establish a Council on International Economic Policy*, 92nd Congress, 2nd Session, May 31, 1972. Washington: U.S. Government Printing Office, 1972, p. 3.
10 Peter G. Peterson, *The United States in the Changing World Economy*, Vol. 1: A Foreign Economic Perspective, 1971, p. 51.
11 Quoted in Dom Bonafede, op. cit., p. 2239.
12 Frank V. Fowlkes, 'Economic Report: Connally Revitalises Treasury Assumes Stewardship of Nixon's New Economic Policy,' *National Journal*, October 2, 1971, p. 1990.
13 Mark L. Chadwin, op. cit., p. 106.
14 Quoted in Michael C. Jensen, 'U.S. Reportedly Withheld Ecuador Aid on I.T.T. Plea,' *New York Times*, August 10, 1973, p. 37. Also see 'When $25,000 stood between ITT and Ecuador,' *Business Week*, August 11, 1973, pp. 102–103.
15 Dan Morgan, 'Officials Say Aid to Ecuador Halted as ITT Bargained,' *Washington Post*, August 10, 1973, p. A2.
16 U.S. Congress, House, Committee on Banking and Currency, Subcommittee on International Finance, *To Provide for Increased Participation by the United States in the International Development Association*, 92nd Congress, 1st Session, July 6, 1971. Washington: U.S. Government Printing Office, 1971, p. 94.
17 Under-Secretary of the Treasury Charles E. Walker, in a letter to House Inter-American Affairs subcommittee chairman Fascell, as quoted in U.S. Congress, House, *New Directions for the 1970's, Part 2: Development Assistance Options for Latin America*, op. cit., p. 116.
18 U.S. Congress, House, *To Provide for Increased Participation by the United States in the International Development Association*, op. cit., p. 101.
19 *Interview No. 2–17*: Washington, D.C., August 13, 1973.
20 U.S. Congress, House, *New Directions for the 1970's, Part 2: Development Assistance Options for Latin America*, op. cit., pp. 113–118. The U.S. government controls approximately one quarter of the votes on the World Bank Board, giving it a virtual veto power over loan decisions—especially when one considers that 'other major shareholders such as West Germany are very anxious to avoid offending it.' See 'Chile: War of Nerves,' *Latin America*, October 20, 1972, p. 335.
21 Quoted in 'Connally's Hard Sell against Inflation,' *Business Week*, July 10, 1971, p. 65.
22 Both Allende and the Chilean Congress deemed 'unacceptable' Kennecott and Anaconda's bigger profits from their Chilean operations as compared to their other operations around the world. See John Strasma, *Some Economic Aspects of Non-Violent Revolution in Chile and Peru, with Emphasis on the Mining and Manufacturing Sectors*, Latin American Studies Association Convention, Austin, Texas, December 1971, p. 17. A decision on the other U.S. copper corporation—Cerro—was held in abeyance.

23 Quoted in Benjamin Welles, 'Chile's Move Spurs U.S. to "Get Tough",' *New York Times,* September 30, 1971, p. 3.

24 Quoted in "U.S. Expects 'Adequate' Chilean Payment for Nationalized Mines," *Wall Street Journal,* September 30, 1971, p. 10.

25 'U.S. Responds to Chilean Decision on Compensation for Expropriation,' *Department of State Bulletin,* November 1, 1971, p. 478. When the Allende government started moving against U.S. interests, it did so as part of a general offensive against private Chilean interests. Copper, however, was an isolated sector, not interlocked with substantial Chilean interests. This explains the incapacity of the U.S. to mobilise internal groups within Chile in support of its position. In response to the Rogers' statement, the Chilean opposition parties publicly declared their full support of the Government's action. 'In matters where the national interest is at stake,' declared the President of the Christian Democratic Party, 'there is no distinction between the Government and Opposition.' Quoted in Juan de Onis, 'Rogers' Stand Spurs Unity Drive in Chile,' *New York Times,* October 15, 1971, p. 3.

26 U.S. Congress, House, Committee on Foreign Affairs, Subcommittee on Inter-American Affairs, *Recent Developments in Chile,* 92nd Congress, 1st Session, October 15, 1971. Washington: U.S. Government Printing Office, 1971, pp. 3–4. An NSC staff member agreed that the payments demanded 'would have hurt the Chilean economy. No doubt about it.' *Interview No. 2–18:* National Security Council, August 14, 1973.

27 *Interview No. 2–15:* U.S. Department of State, July 10, 1973.

28 'Chile-U.S. Clash Over Copper Poses New Threat to Hemisphere,' *Business Latin America,* October 7, 1971, pp. 313–314.

29 See 'Six Concerns Embroiled in Seizure by Chile are Called in by Rogers,' *Wall Street Journal,* October 25, 1971, p. 10; Jeremiah O'Leary, 'U.S. May Halt Aid to Chile in Copper Seizure Action,' *Washington Star,* October 22, 1971, p. A1; Benjamin Welles, 'Rogers Threatens Chilean Aid Cutoff in Expropriation,' *New York Times,* October 23, 1971, p. 1.

30 U.S. Congress, Senate, *Multinational Corporations and United States Foreign Policy, Part 2,* op. cit., pp. 975–979.

31 North American Congress on Latin America, *New Chile,* op. cit., p. 42. According to an ITT memorandum, Anaconda had also got Senator Mansfield 'assisting them in attempting to press for a favourable tax ruling from IRS to take the Chilean loss at an ordinary loss rather than a capital loss.' *Ibid.,* p. 954. U.S. Congress, Multinational Corp., op. cit., Part 2, p 954.

32 *Ibid.,* p. 940.

33 *Ibid.,* p. 971.

34 U.S. Congress, Senate, *Multinational Corporations and United States Foreign Policy, Part 1,* op. cit., pp. 328–329. U.S. public policy linked Chile's creditworthiness to three main criteria: the Allende government's management of the economy, its attitude toward international debt obligations, and its position on the interrelated questions of expropriation and compensation. In practice, however, the notion of creditworthiness has been used to distinguish between political régimes —to contrast them in terms of the kinds of policies adopted towards critical political groups in the society, and as regards their external policies. The severe repression of the masses by the military government in Brazil since 1964, together with the junta's anti-communism

and receptivity to foreign investment contrasted favourably with the national-popular policies of the Goulart period. As a result, U.S. and international lines of credit increased dramatically. The Peruvian military junta's creditworthiness was in part based on its margination of the masses from any effective role in the society. The U.S. government granted $35,573,000 in aid to the right-wing government of Hugo Banzer in Bolivia, which ousted the leftist government of General Torres in August 1971, 'even though the economy was in shambles.' In testimony before a House subcommittee, Herman Kleine, Deputy Coordinator for the Alliance for Progress, gave as one of the reasons for this aid the fact that the conservative counterrevolution had 'improved (the) climate for foreign investment. . . .' See Laurence Stern, 'Aid Used As Choke on Allende,' *Washington Post*, September 19, 1973, p. A14; U.S. Congress, House, Committee on Appropriations, Subcommittee on Foreign Operations and Related Agencies, *Foreign Assistance and Related Appropriations for 1973, Part 1*, 92nd Congress, 1st Session. Washington: U.S. Government Printing Office, 1972, p. 1091.

35 *NACLA's Latin America & Empire Report*, January 1973, p. 15. 'The bankers and exporters interviewed were quick to deny any direct, political pressure to cease giving credits to Chile. However, relations between the Treasury Dept. and the New York banks are on a day-to-day, personal basis and one banker did admit: "We are influenced to a considerable degree by the attitude of the U.S. government—it couldn't be otherwise. We deal with the USSR, with Yugoslavia and China, but not with Chile. Why? Because of the policy of the government." ' *Ibid.*, p. 16.

36 *Facts on File*, August 12–18, 1971, p. 640. In October 1970, when it was clear that Allende would be confirmed as president by the Chilean Congress, the Export-Import Bank immediately reclassified Chile's credit standing from a 'C' to 'D'—the poor risks category. See Economist Intelligence Unit, *Quarterly Economic Review of Chile*, No. 4, December 1970, p. 5.

37 Laurence Stern, 'Aid Used As Choke on Allende,' *Washington Post*, September 10, 1973, p. A1, A14.

38 Marilyn Berger, 'Chile Seeks to Acquire Jets,' *Washington Post*, June 4, 1971, p. A10. Also see testimony of John H. Crimmins, Acting Assistant Secretary of State, before the Senate Foreign Relations Committee. Crimmins attempted to justify the Bank decision while, at the same time, supporting an increase in U.S. military credits to Chile. Committee chairman William Fulbright pointed to the contradictory nature of Crimmins' position:

'I can only emphasise it seems to me a very ironic thing that you even question the sale of a 707 and yet you positively already recommended an increase in military sales. It seems a very odd posture for the United States to be in of even having doubts about giving Chile the right to buy on the usual terms, with the Export Bank which was established for that purpose, a civilian transport which I am sure Boeing is most anxious to sell, and then without any hesitation apparently recommending a $6 million increase in the military sales. This just seems utterly inconsistent to what I thought was our policy.'

U.S. Congress, Senate, Committee on Foreign Relations, *Inter-American Development Bank Funds for Special Operations*, 92nd Congress, 1st Session, June 4, 1971. Washington: U.S. Government Printing Office, 1971, p. 59. The *Washington Post* called the episode 'a major failure of American policy,' and declared that 'no self respecting government, Marxist or otherwise, can be expected to dance a jig for Henry Kearns.' Senator Kennedy called it a 'heavy-handed' policy. See 'Bullying Chile,' *Washington Post*, September 14, 1971, p. A18; Senator Edward M. Kennedy, op. cit., pp. 2–3.

39 'Chile: the Jet Set,' *Latin America*, August 20, 1971, p. 265.

40 Tad Szulc, 'U.S. Retaliating for Foreign Seizures,' *New York Times*, August 14, 1971, p. 3. One White House aide said of the State Department that it 'always tries for a position of perpetual flexibility.' Quoted in Mark L. Chadwin, op. cit., p. 97.

41 Laurence Stern, op. cit., p. A14.

42 *Ibid.*

43 Quoted in International Bank for Reconstruction and Development, International Finance Corporation, International Development Association, 1972 Annual Meetings of the Board of Governors, (*Summary Proceedings*), Washington, D.C., September 25–29, 1972, pp. 58–59.

44 U.S. Congress, House, *To Authorise the United States to Provide Additional Financial Resources to the Asian Development Bank and the Inter-American Development Bank*, op. cit., p. 139. Also see Murray Rossant, 'The Big Stick is Now Economic,' *New York Times*, October 10, 1971, p. E8.

45 Teresa Hayter, *Aid as Imperialism*, Harmondsworth: Pelican Books, 1971, p. 44.

46 Lewis H. Diuguid, 'Schweitzer Gains Backers for IMF in Latin America,' *Washington Post*, October 29, 1972, p. F1.

47 Paul E. Sigmund, op. cit., p. 329. By January 1973, the Allende government had drawn $187.8 million in credits from the IMF. See 'Chile Receives SDR Credit From IMF to Alleviate Country's Payments Problem,' *Business Latin America*, January 25, 1973, p. 31.

48 OAS, Inter-American Social and Economic Council, Inter-American Committee on the Alliance for Progress, op. cit., p. 12.

49 *Ibid.*, p. 148.

50 *Ibid.*, p. 139. The volume of copper production and exports in 1971 was higher than in any year since 1961, but the value of exports declined by 16.2 per cent in relation to 1970 because of a 20.6 per cent decline in the price of copper. See *ibid.*, p. 10.

51 Economist Intelligence Unit, *Quarterly Economic Review of Chile*, No. 2, May 1973, p. 22.

52 Economist Intelligence Unit, *Quarterly Economic Review of Chile*, No. 3, September 1973, pp. 23–24. On the drop in foreign exchange reserves, this source reported in September 1972 that reserves had declined from almost $300 million to around $50 million within the space of just over a year. See Economist Intelligence Unit, *Quarterly Economic Review of Chile*, No. 3, September 1972.

53 Economist Intelligence Unit, *Quarterly Economic Review of Chile*, No. 3, September 1973, pp. 23–24.

54 U.S. Congress, House, Committee on Foreign Affairs, Subcommittee on Foreign Economic Policy, *New Realities and New Directions in*

United States Foreign Economic Policy, 92nd Congress, 1st Session, February 28, 1972. Washington: U.S. Government Printing Office, 1972, p. 21. On the Treasury position, also see Benjamin Welles, 'We Don't Have Any Friends Anyway,' *New York Times*, August 15, 1971, p. E6; Benjamin Welles, 'U.S. Weighs Policy on Expropriation,' *New York Times*, August 22, 1971, p. 11.

55 'President Nixon Issues Policy Statement on Economic Assistance and Investment Security in Developing Nations,' *Department of State Bulletin*, February 7, 1972, pp. 153–154. Also see Richard Nixon, *U.S. Foreign Policy for the 1970's*. A Report to the Congress, February 9, 1972, pp. 990–991.

56 *Interview No. 2–19*: U.S. Department of the Treasury, August 19, 1973. This official also thought that 'the Cuban experience (in the early 1960's) had quite a bit of impact; something that filtered down. Treasury was going to make sure that U.S. investors would be protected if expropriations took place.'
A former policy adviser with the National Security was more critical of this tactic as it affected long-term U.S. economic interests in Latin America:

'The 1972 approach places great emphasis upon the issue of compensation. In fact, the position is that no expropriation is legal, but negative, and something which affects our aid policy and our actions in the international agencies. This is a short-sighted point of view. We have significant interests that go beyond investment interests. . . . This type of policy may be creating harm. It is more important to view this in a broader context. Antagonistic response being applied in cases of expropriation reinforces attitudes, and therefore affects attitudes on a whole range of other issues important to the United States.'

Interview No. 2–16: Washington, D.C., August 9, 1973.

57 *Interview No. 2–21*: U.S. Department of State, August 21, 1973.

58 *Interview No. 2–17*: Washington, D.C., August 13, 1973. The President established a special inter-departmental 'expropriations' committee, chaired by the Assistant Secretary of State for Economic Affairs, National Advisory Council on International Monetary and Financial Policies, *Annual Report*, July 1–June 30, 1972, to the President and to Congress. December 8, 1972, p. 35.

59 Quoted in 'U.S. Policy on Foreign Seizure of Assets Stiffened; Bilateral and Other Aid Curbed,' *Wall Street Journal*, January 20, 1972. p. 5.

60 'The Nixon Warning on Expropriation: What it Will Mean to Companies,' *Business Latin America*, January 27, 1972.

61 *Ibid.*, p. 26.

62 *Interview No. 2–16*: Washington, D.C., August 9, 1973.

63 See U.S. Congress, Senate, Committee on Foreign Relations, House, Committee on Foreign Affairs, *Legislation on Foreign Relations*, Joint Committee Print, March 1973. Washington: U.S. Government Printing Office, 1973, pp. 990-991.

64 *Interview No. 2–19*: U.S. Department of the Treasury, August 19, 1973. In September 1972, the U.S. General Accounting Office made available for publication the unclassified sections of its report on the 'U.S. System for Appraising and Evaluating Inter-American Development Bank Projects and Activities,' dated August 22, 1972. In a section

of the report entitled 'Loans to Countries Involved in Expropriation of Property,' the GAO was apparently highly critical of Treasury policy within IDB. This can be inferred, not from this section of the report which was heavily censored, but from the Treasury Department's response to the still classified sections of the report:

> 'An implicit hard-line, high-profit approach, involving not only a rigid posture in Inter-American negotiations but also in aggressive, confrontational U.S. posture in the working decisions of the Bank underlies this section. In the best judgement of the Treasury it is wrong to equate effective U.S. management with this approach. . . .'

See U.S. Congress, House, Committee on Foreign Affairs, Subcommittee on Inter-American Affairs, *Treasury Department Management of U.S. Participation in the Inter-American Development Bank*, 92nd Congress, 2nd Session (Appendix), September 21, 1972. Washington: U.S. Government Printing Office, 1972, p. 44.

65 Quoted in International Bank for Reconstruction and Development, International Finance Corporation, International Development Association, *Summary Proceedings*, 1973 Annual Meeting of the Board of Governors, Nairobi, Kenya, September 24–28, 1973, Washington, D.C., p. 193.

66 U.S. Congress, House, *To Provide for Additional U.S. Contributions to the Asian Development Bank and the International Development Association*, op. cit., p. 35.

CHAPTER VI

Copper Conflict and the Embargo

The U.S. based multi-national corporation has been in a strategic position in the Chilean economy for over a half century. Chilean dependence and the concomitant decapitalisation of the economy have been sources of economic backwardness and vulnerability. Both features of the Chilean economy have provided the multi-national corporations with political and economic levers with which to limit Chile's efforts at autonomous economic development, blocking imports necessary for copper production as well as exports into foreign markets.

The legacy of Frei's 'Chileanisation' of copper programme was appalling : enormous foreign debts, stagnant production and huge repatriated profit margins. The efforts of the Allende Government to offset these losses and redress the balance between the national and multi-national corporation through nationalisation and compensation based on a retroactive excess profits tax served as the ideological pretext for the U.S. credit and financial restrictions as well as triggering the embargo by the multi-nationals.

Copper policy was critical to any effort aimed at rapid and sustained *national* development—socialist or not. It can also be safely stated that while U.S.-owned copper was the major obstacle to autonomous development, in moving on the copper industry, the Allende Government crystallised U.S. opposition, uniting the efforts of government, banks and corporations.

The Chilean economy's historic dependence on copper has not lessened with time. It continues to account for 60 per cent to 70 per cent of total exports and approximately 80 per cent of total export earnings. In 1970, U.S. corporate holdings in the copper sector accounted for 80 per cent of Chile's copper production. The contribution of the copper industry to the overall development of the Chilean economy has been severely limited by three key factors : the vertically integrated 'enclave' nature of the industry, with refining and fabricating plants located abroad; the use of capital-intensive technology, thus minimising the absorption of labour; and the continued emphasis on the remittance, rather than the reinvestment, of profits.

During the first quarter of the twentieth century, the Chilean copper industry was transformed by the intrusion of a small number of large foreign (especially U.S.) corporations, which eliminated the small producer and proceeded to 'organise(d) technology and capital for the purpose of working low-grade deposits by large-scale capital-intensive methods, for the growing mass market.'[1] In the following two decades, the U.S. copper companies consolidated their control over the industry, which, since 1943, has been in a state of relative stagnation. Between 1943 and 1966, output from the U.S.-owned mines increased at a trend rate of less than 0.5 per cent annually. For the same approximate period (1946–1966) Chile's share of the world primary copper market declined steadily from 19.6 per cent to 12.7 per cent.[2]

Attempts by Chilean governments, in response to nationalist pressures, to institute controls over the copper industry in the 1950's were largely unsuccessful. Increasing demands for the nationalisation of the copper industry became so widespread during the 1960's, however, that the Frei administration informed the copper companies that its proposed 'Chileanisation' policy was the only alternative to more drastic action.[3] Anaconda and Kennecott agreed in 1964 to undertake their first large-scale expansion programme since the initial penetration into the industry, partly for reasons of political necessity, and partly because the expansion of productive capacity at the time coincided with the overall global strategies of both U.S. multinational corporations. Furthermore, the Chilean government's proposed new 20-year tax agreement gave the companies 'some reason to believe that those tax elements which were favourable to them would persist long enough for them to make rational long-term decisions.'[4]

But 'Chileanisation' had no more success than previous attempts to make the U.S. copper interests responsive to the overall needs of the Chilean economy :

'The main aim of "Chileanisation" was to increase benefits to Chile by increasing production. The copper companies were to double output by 1972 in return for decreased taxation and other advantages, including new investment capital provided by Chilean stock purchases of 25 per cent to 51 per cent of the various mines, government loans, and government guaranteed loans negotiated with the Export-Import Bank and other U.S. financial institutions. Incredible as it may seem, a $579 million new investment of borrowed capital between 1966 and 1970 failed to increase production significantly. The copper corporations accumulated $632 million in debts without investing any of their own capital. Their profits, on the other hand, increased substantially due to the "Chileanisation" programme and rising copper prices.'[5]

As the following figures show, copper production in the Gran Minería stagnated between 1966 and 1970, despite these large-scale loans contracted by the copper companies and guaranteed by the Chilean government:

Chile: Copper Production, 1966–1970[6]
(thousands of metric tons)

	1966	1967	1968	1969	1970
Large-scale mining operations	536	520	540	541	571

A detailed study of the 'Chileanisation' programme concluded with the statement that 'at every point in the negotiations . . . the foreign companies were favoured.' The negotiations involving Kennecott's El Teniente mine—the world's largest underground copper mine—was a case in point. 'The terms under which El Teniente was partially nationalised were so generous that Kennecott ended the process of negotiation with a higher benefit-cost ratio than either of the other two foreign companies and Chile was left with practically no net benefits at all.'[7] Between 1965 and 1971, the profits for Anaconda and Kennecott amounted to $426 million and $198 million, respectively.[8]

In December 1970, the Allende government introduced a constitutional amendment into the Chilean Congress to nationalise the U.S.-owned copper mines. The proposed formula for compensation payments to the copper companies included deductions for capital remittances abroad, excess profits, and mine depletion. Between 1915 and 1968, Anaconda and Kennecott combined net profits and depreciation allowances from Chile totalled $2,011 million.

Of this amount, only $378 million was reinvested back into the industry.[9] If we consider only the period 1953 to 1968, the extent of decapitalisation of the Chilean economy by the U.S. copper companies is not diminished. U.S. mining and smelting operations (approximately 90 per cent copper) earned profits of $1,036 million over this fifteen-year period, but reinvestments and new investments totalled a meagre $71 million.[10] The extent of exploitation may be more clearly observed if we locate the Anaconda and Kennecott profits from their Chilean subsidiaries within a comparative context. The contrasts are striking. First, since 1915 'the average dollar of revenue from their Chilean operations consistently yielded a greater surplus than that of their domestic operations, except for a few years in the early 1950's.'[11] Second, and more decisive, are the results obtained from a comparison of the 'world-wide profitability' levels of Anaconda and Kennecott with the rate of return on their Chilean investments. Between 1955 and 1970, Anaconda showed an annual rate of return on its entire global investments of 7.18 per cent, but only 3.49 per cent if Chile is excluded. The rate of return on its Chilean operations alone was 20.18 per cent. Kennecott's global rate of return during this period was 11.63 per cent, and 10 per cent excluding Chile. The figure for its Chilean operations was an astounding 34.84 per cent.[12]

The U.S. government reaction to the Chilean formula for compensation was swift and pointed. Chile was given clear warning that the implementation of this formula would seriously affect U.S.-Chilean relations at the government-to-government level.[13] Undeterred, the Chilean Congress unanimously passed the constitutional amendment in July 1971, and provided for compensation to be fixed by the Controller General within 90 days.

During the last two years of the Frei government, the world price for copper exceeded any other year of the 1960's by at least 10 cents a pound. In 1969, copper sold for 66.56 cents a pound on the world market. In 1970, there was a slight decrease to 64.20 cents a pound. However, during the first two years of the Allende government, the international market price of copper declined steeply, to 49.27 cents a pound in 1971, and to 48.20 cents a pound in 1972. A reversion back to 66.00 cents a pound was forecast for 1973. The Chilean government mining agency, CODELCO, has estimated that for every one cent decline in the world price of copper, the copper exporting country loses some $15 million each year. If we compare the last two years of the Frei period with the *three* years of the Allende government (including the projected 1973 figure) we find that the average yearly price for copper on the international market was 65.38 cents a pound for 1969–1970 as compared to 54.49 cents a pound during 1971–1973. On the basis of the CODELCO estimate above, if the average yearly price for copper from 1969 to 1973 was 65.38 cents a pound, then, the Allende government would have received an extra $490 million.[14]

The Anaconda Company and the Kennecott Copper Corporation reacted strongly to the Chilean Controller General's decision of October 1971, that no compensation should be paid to them for their nationalised mines. Kennecott's President, Frank R. Milliken, asserted his corporation's 'determination to obtain prompt, adequate, and effective compensation for its 49 per cent interest in its El Teniente mine.' According to the corporation the expropriation of the mine 'contravene(d) accepted principles of internationl law.'[15] Anaconda Vice-Chairman William E. Quigley declared that his company 'intend(ed) to follow any legal recourse and defend itself in every way against this arbitrary indemnification by the Chilean government.'[16]

In September 1972, Kennecott decided to cease further legal proceedings in Chile in support of its compensation claims, following the refusal of the Chilean Special Copper Tribunal to review the original decision. Milliken stated that Kennecott would 'pursue in other nations its remedies for the confiscated assets.'[17] Speculation that the corporation might attempt to embargo Chile's copper exports was reinforced by a company letter sent to all importers of Chilean copper claiming 'continued rights to El Teniente copper' and informing them of the company's intention to 'take all such action as may be considered necessary in order to protect our rights, including rights with regard to such copper and/or other metals or products and with regard to their proceeds.'[18] Anaconda, meanwhile, continued to seek redress through the Chilean legal process, but its attention was also turned to 'the possibility of additional actions in jurisdictions outside Chile.'[19] For a country almost totally dependent on copper revenues (which had dropped by $200 million in 1971 as a result of declining world market prices) for her foreign exchange, the entire economy was threatened by the serious consequences of a successful or partially successful embargo.

Kennecott's strategy was subsequently defined by its general counsel and secretary, Pierce N. McCreary, as one of 'seiz(ing) El Teniente copper wherever we find it'—essentially through international legal actions designed to block payments to the Chilean Copper Corporation (CODELCO). In France, for example, a court injunction against payment of a Chilean copper shipment was only rescinded on the understanding that Chile 'set aside an equal amount (in escrow) so that it can be paid to Kennecott in the case that (Chile) is found to owe money to the company.'[20] A Kennecott-requested embargo on a $12.5 million shipment to West Germany, Chile's biggest copper customer, remained in effect for some time. Legal actions aimed at attaching payments for Chilean copper shipments to Britain, Sweden, Italy, Holland, the Netherlands, and other European countries were less successful, but not without impact.[21] The decision of the U.S. copper companies to utilise potential pressure points in Western Europe was necessitated by the overall direction of Chilean copper exports. In 1971, approximately 66 per cent of Chile's total copper exports went to six Western European countries (Belgium, France, West Germany, Italy, Sweden, United Kingdom), while the U.S. market absorbed only 8.5 per cent.[22] 'Psychologically,' observed a U.S. copper trader, '(Kennecott's strategy) has a very nerve-racking effect on anybody who buys Chilean copper. It makes everybody very reluctant to get into contracts using Chilean material because they're afraid of litigation.'[23] Sources within the U.S. copper industry confirmed the development of such a trend among buyers of Chilean copper. A further consequence of Kennecott's global campaign was the suspension of loans previously negotiated by Chile with Canadian and Dutch banks.[24]

During the period of the embargo there was 'a great deal of interaction' between Kennecott executives and U.S. government officials, especially within the National Security Council.[25] The other two key policy making bodies, State and Treasury, were also in regular communication with Kennecott: 'Some of the people in the international section in Treasury kept very close contact with them, and related closely to the State Department in that respect.'[26] Given the close correspondence of purpose and policy, U.S. government denials of complicity in the Kennecott actions appear suspect, especially if one takes account of the cordial relations and excellent communications with the copper corporation during the course of the embargo policy. In a speech to the General Assembly of the United Nations in December 1972, Allende described in great detail the national and international politico-economic aggressions directed against his government by such multinational U.S. corporations as Kennecott and ITT. While refraining from any direct condemnations of the U.S. government itself, he implied that these aggressions could not be separated from a specific context—a context created and fueled by the actions of U.S. policy-makers.[27] These actions manifested themselves most visibly in the policies of the U.S. government regarding credits and loans to Chile.

The Kennecott embargo strategy occurred at a time of intense social and political struggles inside Chile. The organised opposition, with political support from the U.S. government, was attempting to create economic chaos in order to undermine the Allende government and encourage a civilian-military coup. A source close to the copper companies was led to remark that 'Kennecott's legal harassment could be simply part of a bigger drive to bring down President Allende's avowedly Marxist government.'[28]

With the refusal of the Chilean Special Copper Tribunal to reconsider the 'no compensation' decision, and the inability of both Kennecott and Anaconda to force the Chilean government to change its position,[29] the copper companies moved to request reimbursement for their losses from the Overseas Private Investment Corporation (OPIC).

OPIC was established by the Foreign Assistance Act of 1969 as a successor to AID's investment guarantee programme for U.S. corporations operating in 'developing' countries. Its purpose was to insure U.S. investment capital 'against losses from certain specific political risks' including 'loss of investment due to expropriation, nationalisation, or confiscation by the foreign government.'[30] One observer accurately perceived that this decision to give increasing support to the global expansion of the U.S. multinational corporation could be expected to give the latter 'a sense of partnership with the government,' and hence, a belief in its backing in conflicts with foreign governments.[31] During recent congressional hearings on the future of OPIC, Senator Church summed up the impact of OPIC's activities on U.S. government policy : ' . . . once the Government assumes the insurance of the company, the company's interest and that of the Government become identical, and the company can fall back on the Government or threaten to fall back on the U.S. Government whenever it deals with a foreign government . . .'[32]

U.S. government policy, however, is not based on a simple 'identity of interest' whereby it indiscriminately comes to the support of any threatened U.S. economic interest. OPIC policies are formulated on the basis of long-term political and economic considerations, rather than as a reflection of particular economic interests. In the case of Chile, the U.S. government differentiated between individual corporate interests and the requirements of aggregate corporate interests. OPIC did not hesitate to intervene in compensation negotiations between the Allende government and particular U.S. corporations after both parties had reached agreement on payments. In one instance, according to an OPIC memorandum, a U.S. investor agreed to accept a Chilean government compensation offer only to be informed by OPIC that it would not give its consent to such an agreement.[33] OPIC also refused to countenance another offer of less than book value for an insured U.S. property 'because of the implications of the negotiations on impending copper nationalisation legislation.'[34]

The 'private' embargo initiated by the copper corporations complemented the economic pressure generated by U.S. government officials. The close ties between corporation and government reflected the common purposes pursued within different spheres of competence. Through corporate contacts in markets and political ties with U.S. officials the copper embargo became one more ingredient incorporated in the formula to overthrow the Allende Government.

NOTES

1   Norman Girvan, *Copper in Chile*. University of the West Indies, Jamaica: Institute of Social and Economic Research, 1972, p. 59.
2   Keith Griffin, *Underdevelopment in Spanish America*, London: George Allen and Unwin, 1971, p. 152.
3   According to Anaconda vice-chairman William E. Quigley, 'in February 1969, Frei informed Anaconda that as the political situation was developing he was unable to control those elements advocating expropriation. In May Frei said that unless there was renegotiation with Anaconda he would be bound to support an expropriation bill. Mr. Quigley said

that at this point he went to Chile and negotiated night and day until June 26.' See NACLA's, *Latin America & Empire Report*, op. cit., p. 25.

4 Norman Girvan, op. cit., p. 61.
5 James D. Cockcroft, Henry Frundt, Dale L. Johnson, and the Chile Rutgers Research Group, *I.T.T., Multinationals, and Chile*, Unpublished paper, Rutgers University, 1972, p. 10.
6 OAS, Inter-American Economic and Social Council, Inter-American Committee on the Alliance for Progress, op. cit., p. 127.
7 Keith Griffin, op. cit., pp. 172, 164.
8 Chile Research Group, Rutgers University, 'Chile Nationalisation of Copper,' in Dale L. Johnson, ed., *The Chilean Road to Socialism*, New York: Doubleday Anchor, 1973, p. 28.
9 Norman Girvan, op. cit., p. 60.
10 Chile Research Group, Rutgers University, op. cit., p. 28.
11 Norman Girvan, op. cit., p. 60.
12 Address by Carlos Fortin, official of the Chilean Government Copper Corporation (CODELCO), before the American Bar Association, New York, reprinted in CORFO, *Chile Economic News*, June 1, 1973, p. 19. Some idea of the continuing high rate of profit during the 'Chileanisation' period may be gleaned from the following figures: the rate of return on all U.S. investments in the Chilean copper industry in 1967 was 27 per cent. In 1968 it was 26 per cent. The figure for Anaconda in 1969 was 39.5 per cent, while for Kennecott it was 24.1 per cent. See Chile Research Group, Rutgers University, op. cit., p. 28.
13 See Juan de Onis, 'U.S. Warns Chile Her Plan to Take Over Copper Holdings Could Hurt Relations,' *New York Times*, February 1971, p. 2. Although a new U.S. Ambassador to Chile was appointed in April, some months elapsed before the withdrawal of the incumbent U.S. Ambassador Edward Korry. 'The major reason appear(ed) to be the confidence that United States copper companies expressed in Mr. Korry as spokesman before the Chilean Government on United States views.' Juan de Onis, 'U.S. Chilean Relations Running into Serious Snags,' *New York Times*, June 2, 1971, p. 13.
14 Economist Intelligence Unit, *Quarterly Economic Review of Chile*, No. 1, March 1973, p. 16 *and* No. 2, May 1973, p. 14.
15 Quoted in *Facts on File*, October 7–13, 1971, p. 800.
16 See 'The Kennecott White Paper on Chile's Expropriation of the El Teniente Copper Mine,' *Inter-American Economic Affairs*, Spring 1972, p. 37.
17 Quoted in Gerd Wilcke, 'Kennecott to Write off Chile Equity Investment,' *New York Times*, September 8, 1972, p. 45.
18 James J. Nagle, 'Kennecott Acts on Chile Copper,' *New York Times*, October 5, 1972, p. 67.
19 *NACLA's Latin America & Empire Report*, 'Chile: Facing the Blockade,' January 1973, p. 22. Also see Gene Smith, 'Copper Bedeviled by Politics,' *New York Times*, November 5, 1972, p. F1.
20 'Freeze is Lifted on Chile Copper,' *New York Times*, November 30, 1972, p. 63.
21 See 'West German Court Embargoes Shipment of Copper from Chile,' *New York Times*, January 10, 1973, p. 51; David Binder, 'Chile Criticises Kennecott Move,' *New York Times*, January 13, 1973, p. 37. According to one source, Kennecott's actions during early 1973

resulted in losses which forced CODELCO to reassign 5,000 tons of copper to alternative markets. See Economist Intelligence Unit, *Quarterly Economic Review of Chile*, No. 1, March 1970, p. 16.

22 See U.S. Department of the Interior, Bureau of Mines, *Minerals Yearbook, Vol. 1, 1971*. Washington: U.S. Government Printing Office, 1973, p. 494.

23 Quoted in 'Paris Court Bars Payment for Chile Copper at Kennecott's Behest, Clouding the Market,' *Wall Street Journal*, October 5, 1972, p. 38. Furthermore, 'Kennecott's legal offensive (had) been timed for what is known in the trade as "the mating season" when buyers and sellers get together to make their contracts for the following year.' Clyde H. Farnsworth, 'Chile Assailed by Kennecott, Seeks Support,' *Washington Post*, October 17, 1972, p. 55.

24 See 'Chile: War of Nerves,' *Latin America*, October 20, 1972, p. 334.

25 *Interview No. 2–18*: National Security Council, Washington, D.C., August 14, 1973; Also see *Interview No. 2–21*: U.S. Department of State, August 21, 1973.

26 *Interview No. 2–17*: Washington, D.C., August 13, 1973.

27 For the complete text of Allende's speech, see 'Chile: No More Dependence' (Spokesman Pamphlet No. 31) or the Cuban Communist Party newspaper, *Granma*, December 10, 1972, pp. 10–11.

28 Quoted in 'Kennecott Declares War,' *Forbes*, December 1, 1972, p. 27. An international lawyer who was consulted on the company's global strategy was more forthright: 'The suits are bringing Chile to her knees. . . . I predict a real purge.' Quoted in *ibid.*

29 In December 1972, the Chilean Special Copper Tribunal ruled that Cerro Corporation should be paid $37.5 million for its nationalised mine —a figure close to the amount Cerro had claimed. Cerro's satisfactory settlement was apparently the result of three factors: it had begun operations in partnership with the Chilean government; it had not remitted any profits abroad at the time of the Anaconda and Kennecott decisions; and it had continued to supply technical help and assistance in the operation of its nationalised mine. See 'Cerro: The Company That Chile Will Pay,' *Business Week*, December 9, 1972, p. 30.

30 Overseas Private Investment Corporation, *Incentive Handbook—Investment Insurance*, p. 1.

31 Marilyn Berger, 'ITT Refused Chile Offer for Holdings,' *Washington Post*, April 10, 1972, p. A1, A4.

32 U.S. Congress, Senate, Committee on Foreign Relations, Subcommittee on Multinational Corporations, *Multinational Corporations and United States Foreign Policy, Part 3*, 93rd Congress, 1st Session, July 18, 19, 20, 30, 31, August 1, 1973. Washington: U.S. Government Printing Office, 1973, p. 141.

33 U.S. Congress, House, Committee on Foreign Affairs, *The Overseas Private Investment Corporation*, 93rd Congress, 1st Session, Committee Print, September 4, 1973. Washington: U.S. Government Printing Office, 1973, p. 100.

34 From an OPIC memorandum as quoted in *ibid.* In respect of the copper companies, OPIC approved full payment of $11.89 million to Anaconda, and $66.9 million out of a requested $74.4 million by Kennecott. The payment to Kennecott was strongly supported by the Treasury Department *and* the Department of State. The latter submitted a number of

'recommendations' in behalf of Kennecott. See Marcel Niedergang, 'Santiago Takes a Prudent Line,' *Manchester Guardian Weekly* (Le Monde Supplement, December 30, 1972, p. 25.

CHAPTER VII

The Politics of the Foreign Debt

The foreign debt was like an albatross around the neck of the Allende government. Pressured to make payments, denied new loans, eager for financial assistance yet fearful of losing its credit status, the Allende government never publicly entertained the possibility of repudiating its foreign debts. Unlike the case with the credit, financial and trade squeeze, which denied new economic resources to the government, the debt squeeze sought to extract financial resources from Chile. By demanding payments on schedule, U.S. policy-makers had a 'no lose' strategy in mind : if Chile paid up it would have to divert scarce funds from popular programmes and development projects, thus generating political opposition; if Chile did not pay, its international credit rating would decline, new loans from non-U.S. sources would not be forthcoming, and loss of financing of imports would cause an economic decline generating political discontent. Chilean perceptions of the U.S. bargaining position were essentially erroneous : there was no discrete set of issues that could have been negotiated and settled, least of all while U.S.-supported opposition groups in Chile were active and gaining strength. The prolonged and fruitless negotiations ostensibly over the issue of copper compensation was a ploy to which U.S. policy-makers resorted, in order to conceal their more fundamental opposition to the political-economic system which was proposed in Chile. In a word, conflict over debt payments allowed the U.S. to embarrass the Chilean Government by publicising its shaky financial structure in a highly visible manner within an international forum, apply pressure on scarce economic resources, and exacerbate divisions within the Allende coalition.

There were high Chilean officials who eagerly sought an accommodation with the U.S., believed it was possible and were willing to limit socio-economic changes in order to obtain it; and there were those who were less sanguine but who were unable to influence the government's course. The end result was that the U.S. position on the debt, of negotiation and no-settlement, allowed the U.S. to keep the pressure on without appearing to do so.

In November 1971, Allende announced that Chile would ask her foreign creditors in Western Europe and the United States to renegotiate the schedule of payments on debts accumulated, in large part, by the Alessandri and Frei governments. More than half of the approximately $3.83 billion public and private debt as of December 1970 was owed to U.S. government agencies and U.S. private lenders.[1] The 'Paris Club' negotiations were, not surprisingly, 'complicated' by the copper issue. 'It was bound to come up,' observed one U.S. official.[2] In an abrupt departure from traditional practice, the position of leadership of the U.S. delegation at the Paris talks was transferred from the State Department to the Treasury Department. It was felt that Treasury would be more likely to 'keep Chile's feet to the fire,'[3] over the copper expropriations. Despite opposition on the part of Chile's Western European creditors to any discussion on this issue, the U.S. government was insistent that 'progress in one field is tied to progress in the other.'[4]

Previous attempts to reach agreement on the renegotiation of Chile's external debt failed, in part, because of Chile's refusal to accept an International Monetary Fund 'standby' agreement as a requirement for renegotiation :

> 'Chile has opposed such an agreement on the grounds that it means sacrificing autonomy in internal economic policy. Such an agreement would certainly lay down norms concerning wages and prices policy, fiscal and monetary policy, and trade and exchange policy. And this would almost certainly mean an end to the present domestic expansion in Chile, a curbing of government expenditure and credit, and an insistence upon movement toward trade liberalisation and devaluation. The political implications of such policies, enforced from the outside, would be extremely embarrassing for the administration.'[5]

In April 1972, an agreement in principle to renegotiate Chile's debt schedule on a bilateral basis with each creditor nation was concluded. In return, Chile accepted an ambiguous compromise statement of 'just compensation for all nationalisations, in conformity with Chilean and international law.'[6] The creditor nations agreed to reschedule 70 per cent of the interest and principle payments falling due from November 1971 through December 1972, rejecting a Chilean request for an extension until December 1974. Almost three-quarters of the $97 million eligible for rescheduling was owed to the U.S. government, which proceeded to make 'just compensation' for nationalised U.S. assets a precondition for bilateral U.S.-Chilean negotiations.[7] 'At that time,' recalled a high-ranking Treasury official, 'we brought out our concerns on (the Kennecott and Anaconda nationalisations) as being particularly germane to the whole question of creditworthiness and the re-scheduling of debts.'[8]

Chile was able successfully to conclude debt agreements with its Western European creditors without accepting an IMF 'standby' loan as demanded by the United States. However, Chile was unable to moderate the rigid U.S. position on renegotiation, and no bilateral agreement was signed.

Discussions between U.S. and Chilean officials on the debt problem were resumed in late 1972, at a time of intense social and political struggle in Chile. There was no appreciable change in the U.S. position. 'Washington has tied the proposed rescheduling,' wrote *Business Week*, 'to a settlement on expropriated U.S. proper-ties.'[9] That the Chileans were increasingly concerned to resolve this critical problem was not in doubt. Even the CIA, who were now represented on the U.S. delegation, agreed on this point:

'It was our judgement that the (Chileans) were interested in working out some kind of modus vivendi without, however, retreating substantially from their position.'[10]

CIA representation on the negotiating team, occurring at a time of active CIA involvement in the promotion of anti-government demonstrations in Chile, reflected the U.S. decision to accelerate pressures on the Allende government to bring about its downfall.

In February 1973, Allende expressed his willingness to submit the copper dispute to an international commission for resolution, pursuant to a 1914 bilateral treaty between the U.S. and Chile (Brian Treaty) for the peaceful settlement of disputes. The *Economist Intelligence Unit* called the proposal 'an indication of how the United States is increasingly linking the question of the renegotiation of Chile's foreign debt and renewed credit facilities to the question of just and swift compensation for the expropriated American copper companies.' The U.S. refusal to compromise and its rejection of the international tribunal was based on a policy of permanent confrontation. To compromise with Chile and reach an agreement would have weakened the internal opposition. In these circumstances, it is not surprising that a new round of bilateral talks in March 1973 ended abruptly 'without any shred of hope that the dialogue will be continued in a friendly fashion.'[12] Chilean policymakers, nonetheless, continued in their efforts to devise a satisfactory compromise based on the assumption that the U.S. position was still based on the idea that 'Chile has got to recognise the connection between copper and debt rescheduling as related subjects.'[13] In fact the U.S. government's posture, however, had hardened beyond compromise.

NOTES

1   See Economist Intelligence Unit, *Quarterly Economic Review of Chile*, Annual Supplement, 1973, p. 15. The external public debt was put at $3.17 billion and the external private debt at $659,000. The estimated total debt for 1971 was approximately $3.62 billion. The World Bank figure for Chile's external public debt as of December 31, 1970—approximately $2.5 billion—seriously understates the extent of Chile's indebtedness under the Frei government. See World Bank, *Annual Report 1972*, p. 83 and World Bank Group, *Trends in Developing Countries*, 1973, Table 4.6. In March 1973, Acting Assistant Secretary of State for Inter-American Affairs John H. Crimmins estimated that the U.S. held 55 per cent of Chile's debt to public agencies and 36 per cent of the debt to private lenders. See U.S. Congress, House Committee on Foreign Affairs, Subcommittee on Inter-American Affairs, *United States–Chilean Relations*, 93rd Congress, 1st Session, March 6, 1973. Washington: U.S. Government Printing Office, 1973, p. 4.

2   Quoted in 'Chile: Its Credit Rating is at Stake,' *Business Week*, January 29, 1972, p. 37. Also see Juan de Onis, 'Chile, Reserves Low, Will Seek Renegotiation of Payments on Her $3 Billion Foreign Debt,' *New York Times*, November 10, 1971, p. 12; Everett G. Martin, 'Chile Meets with International Creditors to Renegotiate Payments on $1.3 Billion,' *Wall Street Journal*, January 10, 1972, p. 5; Juan de Onis, 'Chile, $3 Billion in Debt, Asks Creditors to Accept Moritorium on Payments,' *New York Times*, January 20, 1972, p. 4.

3   Quoted in Rowland Evans and Robert Novak, 'Rocky May Get State Department,' *Washington Post*, February 7, 1972, p. A19.

4   *Interview No. 2–15*: U.S. Department of State, July 10, 1973.

5   Economist Intelligence Unit, *Quarterly Economic Review of Chile*, No. 1, March 1972, p. 5.

6　John L. Hess, 'U.S. Joins in Credit Accord with Chile,' *New York Times*, April 20, 1972, p. 3. The U.S. government had originally wanted the phrase 'prompt, adequate, and effective' compensation accepted by the Chileans. See 'Chile: Prop for Socialism,' *Latin America*, April 28, 1972, p. 129.

7　U.S. Congress, House, Committee on Appropriations, Subcommittee on Foreign Operations and Related Agencies, *Foreign Assistance and Related Agencies Appropriations for 1973, Part 1*, 92nd Congress, 1st Session. Washington: U.S. Government Printing Office, 1972, pp. 1095–1096.

8　John Hennessy, Assistant Secretary of the Treasury for International Affairs, as quoted in U.S. Congress, Senate, Committee on Foreign Relations, Subcommittee on Multinational Corporations, *Multinational Corporations and United States Foreign Policy, Part 1*, op. cit., p. 331. See also 'U.S. Links Payments, Chile Talks,' *Washington Post*, July 24, 1972, p. A3.

9　'Kennecott Collects on Its Insurance,' *Business Week*, December 23, 1972, p. 26. Also see 'U.S. and Chile Begin Talks on Rifts,' *New York Times*, December 21, 1972; Terri Shaw, 'U.S.–Chile Discussions Adjourned After 3 Days,' *Washington Post*, December 23, 1972, p. A16.

10　Secret testimony of CIA director Wiliam E. Colby and a senior official in the CIA's Office of Current Intelligence, before the House Subcommittee on Inter-American Affairs on October 11, 1973, as quoted in Tad Szulc, op. cit., p. C5.

11　Economist Intelligence Unit, *Quarterly Economic Review of Chile*, No. 2, May 1973, p. 23.

12　'Chile: Financial Confrontation,' *Latin America*, April 6, 1973, pp. 105–106.

13　*Interview No. 2–21*: U.S. Department of State, August 21, 1973. To the end, Chilean policymakers accepted the U.S. public position without question:

> 'Although high-ranking members of the Allende govt. repeatedly alleged that large amounts of dollars were entering Chile to pay for strikes and anti-Allende campaigns, they never substantiated their claims in public. Three weeks before the coup, I raised the question of "foreign financing" in separate interviews with a senior member of the secret service and with a close aide of Allende. Both men declined to disclose any details "for policy reasons".

> "We are presently negotiating our debt with Washington," Allende's aide said. "These negotiations are vital to us, and we cannot afford a scandal now".'

See Marlisle Simons, op. cit., p. B3.

CHAPTER VIII

U.S. Military Activity, the Coup and the Military Regime

From Congressional testimony of high military and civilian authorities it is clear that the U.S. military possessed extensive contacts among high Chilean officials, and were aware that their relationships were amenable to political influence and manipulation. U.S. military officials were convinced that restraint should be thrown to the wind and that the U.S. should do everything in its power to stop and reverse the socialisation of Chile. There are some indications that a pre-election coup was in the making but that plans went awry. Not able to prevent Allende from coming to power, U.S. policy-makers combined a policy of economic pressures against the Allende Government with selective aid directed toward the military. U.S. policy sought and succeeded in disaggregating the Chilean state—essentially establishing links with the military which in turn captured the state, purged all dissidents and pursued a development policy within the 'market' framework embraced by the Nixon Administration.

Between 1950 and 1969, U.S. military assistance to Latin America, in the form of equipment, training and services, totalled $1.357 billion.[1] In addition, there were visible examples of direct and indirect U.S. military intervention—Guatemala (1954), Cuba (1961), Dominican Republic (1965)—in support of U.S. economic interests threatened by the policies of moderate and radical nationalist political groupings. However, beginning in the early 1960's, a transformation in U.S. defence policy regarding the hemisphere began to take place. The emphasis shifted from a concern over the possibilities of external military intervention by a non-hemispheric power to a concern over the threat to the political and economic status quo represented by internal insurgency, particularly guerrilla movements. 'The free world's security,' declared President Kennedy, 'can be endangered not only by a nuclear attack but also by being slowly nibbled away at the periphery, regardless of our strategic power, by forces of subversion, infiltration, intimidation, indirect or non-overt aggression, internal revolution, lunatic blackmail, guerrilla warfare or a series of limited wars.'[2] In 1965, the director of the Military Assistance Programme during the Johnson Administration, General Robert Wood, asserted that :

'. . . the primary purpose of the proposed fiscal year 1965 Military Assistance Programme for Latin America is to counter the threat to the entire area by providing equipment and training which will bolster the internal security capabilities of the recipient countries.'[3]

Nonetheless, the Kennedy and Johnson Administrations engaged in both covert and overt military activities in Latin America, and the Nixon policy of 'low profile' or, more accurately, *indirection*, was essentially rooted in the conviction that direct military intervention would have a negative impact on U.S. political and economic interests in the hemisphere given the present conjuncture of events. However, wariness over the consequences of military intervention in a period of rising economic nationalism was accompanied by a policy which stressed 'a very close relationship between the prospects for achieving social and economic reform and development goals and a necessary level of internal security and stability.'[4] Secretary of Defence Melvin Laird described in detail this policy of consolidating and improving the counter-insurgency capabilities of U.S.-oriented régimes in the area, in March 1970 :

'The basic policy of decreasing direct U.S. military involvement cannot be successful unless we provide our friends and allies, whether through grant aid or credit sales, with the material assistance necessary to insure the most effective possible contribution by the manpower they are willing and able to commit to their own and the common defence. Many of them simply do not command the resources or technical capabilities to assume greater responsibility for their own defence without such assistance. The challenging objectives of our new policy can, therefore, be best achieved when each partner does its share and contributes what it best can to the common effort. In the majority of cases, this means indigenous manpower organised into properly equipped and well-trained armed forces with the help of material, training, technology and specialised skills furnished by the United States through the Military Assistance Programme or as Foreign Military Sales.'[5]

The report of a special Congressional study mission to Latin America in early 1970, to assess the military assistance training programme, was more direct :

'In conclusion, the study mission wishes to point out that the majority of issues which must be addressed about MAP training are political and economic in nature, rather than strictly military. This emphasis reflects our strong convictions that military assistance programmes are primarily an instrument of American foreign policy and only secondarily of defence policy.'[6]

A staff memorandum prepared later that year for the Senate Foreign Relations Committee, on U.S. military assistance and U.S. AID public safety programmes in Guatemala and the Dominican Republic, suggested that this indeed was the basis for U.S. military aid to the hemisphere. It was highly critical of the 'political price' involved in maintaining these programmes in authoritarian and client Latin countries. The study concluded its analysis of the Dominican Republic programme with the observation that 'When all of the rhetoric is stripped away, the basic justification for the military assistance programme is that the programme provides an excuse for the MAAG (Military Assistance Advisory Group) and the MAAG keeps in touch with what the Dominican military are thinking.'[7]

The U.S. response to the overthrow of the nationalist Torres government in Bolivia in August 1971 by a right-wing military coup offers an excellent example of the way in which military aid has been utilised for political and economic ends by the Nixon Administration. After testifying before the House Appropriations Subcommittee in April 1972 on foreign assistance appropriations for fiscal year 1973, General George M. Seignious II, Deputy Assistant Secretary of Defence for International Security Affairs, engaged in debate with Subcommittee chairman Otto Passman :

General Seignious. 'The best example of our military grant aid material going into Latin America is Bolivia. That is where the largest programme is $4.8 million. There is a President now in Bolivia that is somewhat U.S.-oriented and he is faced with dissident elements both internally and externally. . . .

General Seignious. 'We feel that is in the national interest to strengthen the current régime in Bolivia to maintain internal security.
Mr. Passman. 'Our national interest or Bolivia's national interest?'
General Seignious. 'We feel it is in the interest of both Bolivia and the United States.'
Mr. Passman. 'Make the case for the United States, if you will.'
General Seignious. 'We have now, in Bolivia, a country that is at least nominally oriented toward the United States. We feel that for the small expenditure of support in the way of grant aid that that Government can defeat or deny the extension of the insurgency.'[8]

Since 1969, occasional difference and tensions over specific issues with Latin American countries under military rule has led to temporary or short-term conflicts with the United States. Nevertheless, the U.S. has continued to stress the importance of maintaining channels of influence and direction with the Latin American military as one of the major instruments of social control and preservation of the dominant political élites and economic ruling classes in the region. A high level Defence Department policymaker outlined the rationale behind U.S. military assistance policy toward Latin America :

'We are furnishing assistance in the form of military training to almost all of the countries of Latin America. It is sometimes difficult to sort out those that have elected governments from those that don't. We feel it is extremely important to maintain our relations with the people who are in positions of influence in those countries so we can help to influence the course of events in those countries.'[9]

The U.S. Southern Command has a very clear conception of its political tasks in pursuit of U.S. politico-economic interests in Latin America. During questioning of General George R. Mather, U.S. Army, Commander in Chief, U.S. Southern Command, by the

House Foreign Affairs Subcommittee on Inter-American Affairs, in 1970, a highly suggestive discussion occurred :

Mr. Fascell. 'That report that we referred to stressed the theme that your command played a very important or significant political role, and stressed the fact in describing that, that since most of the leaders in Latin America were military men that military men in SOUTHCOM could best deal with them. This was the emphasis of the political aspects of SOUTHCOM. So you personally conceive of your command as playing any kind of a political role in South America either in that aspect or some other aspect?'
Mr. Gross. 'Or your staff?'
General Mather. 'Directly; no. I want to answer that question very, very carefully, Mr. Chairman. First of all, it is a fact, I believe, that the military in Latin America play a very definite role in the political process.'
Mr. Fascell. 'I think we could take judicial notice of that fact.'
General Mather. 'OK. Given that, then, I have an excellent channel to that very important element in this political process.'
Mr. Fascell. 'Do you mean through your MIL Groups in these 17 countries?'
General Mather. 'Exactly. This can be of significant assistance in the conduct of our relations in support of our national purpose. Now, to that extent there is a political aspect to this relationship.'
Mr. Fascell. 'Do you mean as a base of direct communication?'
General Mather. 'This is right.'
Mr. Fascell. 'I mean in the political process of the local country?'
General Mather. 'Yes, as a means of information and communication for the use of our Ambassadors. The MIL Group contacts have, on occasion and for short periods, been the best channel open.'[10]

General Mather was also questioned on the issue of U.S. government support for authoritarian military régimes in Latin America. He viewed such support as 'so important to our national security that we should be prepared to, somehow or other, live with the excesses of which many of them are accused (Security deletion).' He equated U.S. national security interests with the prevention of 'another Cuba,' which prompted Subcommittee Chairman Fascell to raise the issue of the nature of the U.S. response to a 'hypothetical' Communist electoral victory in Chile—only a matter of weeks prior to the 1970 national election in Chile, where a coalition of leftist political forces were given a good chance of obtaining the presidency. 'I don't see,' Fascell declared, 'how the United States could have a direct military response to that event.' The exchange continued:

> *General Mather.* 'I don't either, Mr. Chairman. I just hope that it doesn't happen. As you know, our record of recovery of countries that have gone down the drain is practically nil. We haven't gotten any of them back once they have gone. This is what we have got to stop.'
> *Mr. Fascell.* 'What you are saying here is, that we, as a government, ought to take every action we can which would prevent such an occurrence. Particularly since we are limited in our capability to react?'
> *General Mather.* 'Yes, sir.'[11]

These exchanges appear to have been in keeping with the general tenor of U.S. policy regarding the forthcoming Chilean election in September 1970. Since January, the U.S. Navy had made applications for Chilean visas for 87 officers and civilian employees. Chilean government inquiries regarding this phenomenon elicited a series of contradictory responses from the Defence Department and the Department of State. An explanation that the visas were for a goodwill Navy band tour surprised Chilean officials 'because there was no record that such a visit was planned (and) the ranks of the men involved made it unlikely that they were musicians.' A number of the officers held academic degrees in physics, space, aero-engineering, computer science, and marine biology. Several were navy aviators qualified as destroyer and submarine commanders 'and at least one took graduate studies in defence intelligence . . .' The Chilean Embassy was subsequently informed by the State Department that 49 of the visas were actually for U.S. personnel involved in the coming joint annual anti-submarine warfare exercises. Yet, Chile had officially decided not to participate in these exercises some months previously in order 'to avoid the possibility that the presence of American warships in Chilean waters would be interpreted as a sign of United States political pressure.' U.S. officials did not offer any clarification on this point. The State Department had also maintained that a further 38 visas were for U.S. Antarctic personnel to travel to the U.S. installation at Palmer Base, which is supplied through the Chilean port of Punta Arenas. According to the U.S. Navy, however, the normal complement of base personnel is 10 men. It should be noted, in conclusion, that all the officers for whom visas were requested were classified as 'unrestricted line officers'—which designated them available for any type of duty.[12]

Immediately after Allende's inauguration as President, General Mather, in his capacity as head of the U.S. Southern Command, held discussions with the leaders of the Chilean armed forces. He emphasised, however, that this action 'does not in any way imply a circumvention of the Ambassador nor his responsibility there, since my entire effort and that of my military group is in conjuncture with his overall responsibility.'[13]

In mid-1971, against the background of an emerging aggressive foreign economic policy regarding countries expropriating U.S. economic assets—directed primarily at the Allende government—the United States decided to grant a Chilean request for $5 million in military credits as part of its 'pragmatic policy.'[14] Secretary of State Rogers noted that 'it is quite interesting that in the case of Latin America we are still providing some military assistance to Chile, for the reasons we think it would be better not to have a complete break with them.'[15] In December 1972, the U.S. government announced that a $10 million credit agreement for the Chilean military, signed in May, would be granted—notwithstanding the January 1972 policy statement on aid to governments expropriating U.S.-owned properties without prompt, adequate, and effective compensation.[16] The House Appropriations Subcommittee on foreign assistance, through its chairman Otto Passman, took a highly critical view of this military assistance to Chile during hearings on the 1974 foreign assistance appropriations. The officials being questioned were Vice-Admiral Ray Peet, Director of the Defence Security Assistance Agency and Deputy Assistant Secretary of Defence (International Security Affairs) for Security Assistance, and Curtis W. Tarr, Deputy Under-Secretary of State for coordinating security assistance programmes :

Mr. Passman. 'First let us take Chile. How can you justify an aid programme in Chile?'
Admiral Peet. 'From a Defence Department point of view, we

consider Chile a political problem and therefore primarily a matter of state interest. ———. ———.'

Mr. Passman. 'Let us get back to the basics. You are talking about a Communist form of government.'

Admiral Peet. 'In Chile, yes, sir.'

Mr. Passman. 'They expropriated all the American company properties, did they not? Could a country be any more Communist than Chile?'

Admiral Peet. 'I would prefer that State answer that question.'

Mr. Passman. 'Could they? Do you know of any country that could be any more Communist than Chile?'

Mr. Tarr. 'Mr. Chairman. I think you are right. The problem here is the orientation of the government and the hope is to ———.'

Mr. Long. 'Buy them off.'

Mr. Tarr. '———.'

Mr. Passman. 'How could they get any closer to communism than they are?'

Admiral Peet. 'They can't. However, we are maintaining influence; ———.'[17]

As early as April 1970, the U.S. government had been considering the possibility of employing its waiver power under section 4 of the Foreign Military Sales Act in order to sell jet aircraft to a number of Latin American countries, including Chile. Concern was expressed over countries finding alternative sources of supply and over 'the cost to our political relations with these countries of our continued inability to supply aircraft which they consider reasonable and necessary for the modernisation of their forces.'[18] In May 1973, President Nixon decided to exercise the waiver authority to allow five Latin American countries, including Chile, to purchase F-5E military fighter aircraft, on the grounds that such action was 'important to the national security of the United States.'[19]

On September 11, 1973, a military coup overthrew the democratic socialist government of Chile. 'The Chilean armed forces and carabineros,' declared a military junta communique, 'are united to initiate the historic and responsible mission to fight for the liberation of the fatherland from the Marxist yoke . . .'[20] Former President Eduardo Frei and influential sectors of the Christian Democratic Party voiced their unqualified support for the coup.

The Party's governing council issued an official statement which asserted that the Allende government 'was preparing to stage a violent coup . . . in order to install a Communist dictatorship. Everything indicates that the armed forces did nothing more than to respond to this immediate risk.'[21] Having laid the basis for the coup it was not surprising that the U.S. was unwilling to protest publicly against the violent and unconstitutional overthrow of an elected government. Through its strategically placed officials, agents and operatives active in Chile the U.S. government received advance knowledge of the coup. Yet for propaganda purposes, policy-makers decided to maintain a posture of non-involvement: '. . . Washington at "the highest level" decided on a hands-off policy after evaluating the information . . . this meant that President Nixon was notified.'[22] After the first day of the coup when it became apparent that direct U.S. military intervention would not be necessary, the White House began its campaign denying any U.S. involvement in the coup.[23] The latter position was forcefully stated by Jack Kubisch, Assistant Secretary of State for Inter-American Affairs, in testimony before the House Foreign Affairs Subcommittee on Inter-American Affairs:

> 'I wish to state as flatly and as categorically as I possibly can that we did not have advance knowledge of the coup that took place on September 11 . . . there was no contact whatsoever by the organisers and leaders of the coup directly with us, and we did not have definite knowledge of it in advance.
> 'In a similar vein, either explicitly or implicitly, the U.S. government has been charged with involvement or complicity in the coup. This is absolutely false. As official spokesmen of the U.S. Government have stated repeatedly, we were not involved in the coup in any way.'[24]

As we have shown above, Washington did indeed play a crucial role in establishing the political and social conditions for the coup through its economic policies. Moreover, the relative lack of detailed factual information on U.S. involvement in the coup must be situated within the context of a political system where covert politics plays a vital role. The exact role of the U.S. in the mechanics of the execution of the military aspects of the coup can only be inferred from scanty evidence. What is clear however is that the divergence between public statements and covert actions has been a characteristic of U.S. policy toward the Allende government from the beginning. Kubisch's statement categorically denying U.S. complicity in the coup was followed by a refusal to deny U.S. government financing of the activities of various opposition groups to the Allende government in the pre-coup period. He offered to discuss the matter in closed executive session so as not 'to give a misleading impression abroad . . .'[25]

The secret testimony of William E. Colby, Director of the Central Intelligence Agency, offers a striking contrast to the professed U.S. public position of non-involvement in the internal social and political struggles in Chile leading up to the coup.

Under questioning by the House Foreign Affairs Subcommittee, he implied direct CIA involvement in fomenting internal conflict and the general societal crisis that resulted :

Mr. Harrington. 'Did the CIA, directly or indirectly, assist these (anti-Allende) demonstrations through the use of subsidiaries of United States corporations in Brazil or other Latin American countries?'

Mr. Colby. 'I think I have said that CIA did not assist the trucking strike.'

Mr. Harrington. 'I think it's a broader, and more intentionally broader, question—any of the demonstrations that are referred to in the course of this questioning.'

Mr. Colby. 'I am not quite sure of the scope of that question.'

Mr. Harrington. 'I make specific references to two, one in the October period of 1972 and one in March 1973.'

Mr. Colby. 'I would rather not answer the question than give you an assurance and be wrong. Frankly, I would rather not. If we did, I don't want to be in a position of saying we didn't. But if we didn't, I really don't mind saying I won't reply because it doesn't hurt. But I don't want to be in a position of giving you a false answer. Therefore, I think I better just not answer that, although I frankly don't know the answer to that question right here as I sit here.'[26]

Colby refused to answer questions as to whether the CIA continued its activities in Chile after Allende's inauguration as President in November 1970 :

'If I might comment, the presumption under which we conduct

this type of operation is that it is a covert operation and that the United States hand is not to show. For that reason we in the executive branch restrict any knowledge of this type of operation very severely and conduct procedures so that very few people learn of any type of operation of this nature.'[27]

But, under question by subcommittee chairman Fascell, he explicitly alluded to the ongoing nature of CIA covert operations:

Mr. Fascell. 'Is it reasonable to assume that the Agency has penetrated all of the political parties in Chile?'

Mr. Colby. 'I wish I could say yes. I cannot assure you all, because we get into some splinters.'

Mr. Fascell. 'Major?'

Mr. Colby. 'I think we have an intelligence coverage of most of them. Let's put it that way.'

Mr. Fascell. 'Is that standard operating procedure?'

Mr. Colby. 'It depends on the country. For a country of the importance of Chile to the United States' decision-making, we would try to get an inside picture of what is going on there.'[28]

From these accounts and from the peculiar circumstances surrounding the behaviour of U.S. officials one is led to the conclusion that the U.S. government played an important role in the highly organised and coordinated military operation that culminated in the overthrow of the Allende government. The U.S. Ambassador to Chile, Nathaniel Davis, returned to Washington for discussions with Secretary of State-designate Kissinger and a special 'Chile' group within the National Security Council, and then rejoined the U.S. Embassy staff in Santiago—during the week preceding the coup. The same 'group' which designed the general policy of opposing Allende and which perhaps had been responsible for shifting the timetable for the military coup. On the day the coup took place, four U.S. Navy vessels were headed for Chile to engage in joint hemispheric manoeuvres but, according to the State Department, were re-routed once news of the conflict was received.[29] Subsequently it was determined that a number of U.S. Navy officers were in Valparaiso and in contact with the Naval officers who initiated the coup.

A Congressional subcommittee inquiring into the events surrounding the military coup in Chile, and the activities of U.S.

military personnel, with Assistant Secretary of State Kubisch does not provide much in the way of substantive information nor does it describe accurately the close ties and political perspectives of the U.S. and Chilean military officials.[30]

The State Department took the same tack of admitting extensive interaction between U.S. civilian and military personnel, and the Chilean military; but placed their relations within a 'routine', 'normal', bureaucratic setting, thus attempting to obscure possible political ties.[31]

An account of the activities of U.S. military and civilian personnel in the port city of Valparaiso prior to, and during, the coup suggests that these 'contacts' were not limited to 'routine' duties. The report, authorised by Charles E. Horman, a U.S. resident in Chile subsequently killed by the junta, quoted a retired U.S. engineer formerly stationed in the Panama Canal Zone as saying : 'We came down to do a job and it's done.'[32]

The U.S. decision (September 25) to maintain diplomatic relations with the new military junta was the result of a secret conference between Ambassador Davis and Secretary of State Kissinger, held 'reportedly to discuss means by which the United States can come speedily to the aid of the junta.'[33] The U.S. government was 'the first to make financial overtures' in the form of a Department of Agriculture $24 million credit for the purchase of 'desperately needed wheat,' followed by a further $28 million credit for the purchase of corn.[34] The *Journal of Commerce* called the three-year wheat credit 'extraordinary' in view of prior U.S. policy which had been based on Chile's supposed lack of 'creditworthiness.'[35] Senator Kennedy noted that the wheat credit '(was) eight times the total commodity credit offered to Chile in the past three years when a democratically elected government was in power.'[36] Prior to the coup, a Chilean agricultural trade delegation had attempted —unsuccessfully—to obtain emergency wheat credits from the U.S. government. Pedro Bosch, the purchasing agent for the delegation, remarked at the time that such credits were fundamentally dependent on a 'political decision of the White House . . .'[37]

The junta, for its part, discarded completely the Allende government's nationalist foreign policy, became unconditional supporters of U.S. policies and business interests and outlined a new development strategy designed to encourage foreign capital investment. These political measures re-established Chile's international 'creditworthiness'. The junta severed diplomatic and economic relations with Cuba, gave notice of its intention to play a less dynamic role within the Andean Pact and in regard to such issues as the 200-mile fishing rights dispute and was the most energetic defender of the U.S. at the Foreign Ministers' Meeting in Mexico in 1974. The vast majority of foreign and domestic enterprises intervened in or nationalised during the preceding three years were returned to their original owners, and the junta agreed in principle to paying compensation to the U.S. copper companies.[38]

In light of these measures taken by the junta, the foreign private banking community and the multilateral financial institutions reversed their policies and offered support to the badly battered Chilean economy. *Business Latin America* observed, somewhat caustically, that the major justification for Chile's 'three years of almost total ostracism' by the international banking community continued to exist despite the change in government :

'The bankers' quick response to the junta's plea for "a little Marshall Plan" is something of a mystery. For one thing, the military cried out that the economy was on the brink of bankruptcy when it took over. Moreover, the renegotiation of Chile's onerous *past* foreign debt, now estimated to total $4 billion, has yet to take place. Until that problem is solved, the question of Chile's creditworthiness, which was attacked by the international banking community during the Allende régime, remains unanswered.'[39]

The availability of loans from U.S. private banks to Chile increased almost immediately after the junta took power. Whereas lines of short-term commercial credit had hovered at around $300 million during the Alessandri-Frei years, by the end of 1971, they had declined to $25 to $30 million. Since the coup, the predictions that 'these lines of credit could . . . eventually climb to the levels they had reached before Allende took office'[40] have been amply confirmed in practice. During the first month of junta rule, approximately $200 million in new lines of credit were extended, primarily by U.S. banks.[41] These credits were short-term commercial credits enabling the government to meet its immediate obligations and to purchase products esential to the day-to-day functioning of the Chilean economy.

The international agencies took up the slack in the area of credits for long-term development projects. Missions from the World Bank, the International Monetary Fund, the Inter-American Development Bank, and the Inter-American Committee for the Alliance for Progress (CIAP) 'flocked to Santiago' and, according to Central Bank president General Eduardo Cano, appeared 'well-disposed' towards the junta.[42] The Inter-American Development Bank actually approved an $8.5 million loan to CORFO for a rural electrification programme before its Mission study was completed. It was also considering further development credits in excess of $100 million. The World Bank has already granted $13.5 million to the junta, and has agreed to provide CORFO with an estimated $10.5 million for preinvestment studies in mining, metallurgy, manufacturing, transportation, etc. The International Monetary Fund approved a 'standby' agreement in February 1974 amounting to $95 million. It has been estimated that a decision by IMF Mission that Chile is now 'creditworthy' could result in up to $158 million in 'standby' credits.[43]

In December 1973, the U.S. government agreed to renegotiate part of Chile's foreign debt to U.S. government agencies, after the military junta 'made statements about compensation (for the expropriated U.S. copper companies) that indicated they were serious about it.' Under the terms of the renegotiation, Chile agreed to pay $60 million over a four-year period and a further $64 million over a six-year period beginning in January 1975.[44] The fact remains, however, that the agreement was secured *prior* to a compensation settlement with the copper companies. Previously, U.S. policy makers, both in the 'Paris Club' meetings and in bilateral U.S.-Chilean discussions, had made this a precondition for any renegotiation of Chile's foreign debt. One consequence of this changed U.S. position was the decision of the Export-Import Bank to reconsider its lending policy towards Chile.[45]

The U.S. government policy of prolonged confrontation with the Allende government in order to undermine its capacity to govern, and effect its demise, originated from within the offices of Henry Kissinger and the National Security Council. The NSC located the Allende electoral victory in terms of its future negative impact on U.S. political and economic goals in Latin America, and then proceeded to decentralise the implementation of the overall strategy among the appropriate government agencies. At the critical conjuncture, however, it returned to centre stage to give its final approval. The military coup followed.

The Chilean coup eliminated the core threat to continued U.S. hegemony in Latin America. The restoration of a client régime in Chile had immediate short-term consequences. In October, Secretary of State Kissinger called for a 'new dialogue' between the United States and Latin America to re-examine the nature of the relationship. U.S. officials stated that 'this was (Kissinger's) first policy statement on Latin America and was meant to signal the start of a major effort by the Administration to work out a fresh approach to the problems in the hemisphere . . .'[46] The likelihood of a U.S.-Brazilian 'co-prosperity' policy in Latin America is likely. Chile is merely one of the pieces within this larger picture.

NOTES

1 Michael T. Klare, *War Without End*. New York: Vintage Books, 1972, p. 280.
2 Willard F. Barber and C. Neale Ronning, *Internal Security and Military Power*. Ohio: Ohio University Press, 1966, p. 31.
3 *Ibid.*, p. 35.
4 Testimony of Assistant Secretary of State Meyer, U.S. Congress, Senate, Committee on Foreign Relations, Subcommittee on Western Hemisphere Affairs, *United States Military Policies and Programmes in Latin America*, 91st Congress, 1st Session, June 24 and July 8, 1969. Washington: U.S. Government Printing Office, 1969, pp. 58–59.
5 U.S. Congress, House, Subcommittee of the Committee on Appropriations, *Foreign Assistance and Related Agencies Appropriations for 1971, Part 1*, 91st Congress, 2nd Session. Washington: U.S. Government Printing Office, 1970, p. 307. A succinct statement on one aspect of this policy was provided by G. Warren Nutter, Assistant Secretary of Defence for International Security Affairs in December of same year: 'Our ability to reduce U.S. commitments abroad, and generally to lower our profile, will depend upon the calibre of training we are able to provide to foreign military personnel.' See U.S. Congress, House, Committee on Foreign Affairs, Subcommittee on National Security Policy and Scientific Development, *Military Assistance Training*, 91st Congress, 2nd Session, October 6, 7, 8, December 8 and 15, 1970. Washington: U.S. Government Printing Office, 1970, p. 132.
6 U.S. Congress, House, Committee on Foreign Affairs, Subcommittee on National Security Policy and Scientific Developments, *Report of the Special Study Mission to Latin America on 1. Military Assistance Training and 11. Developmental Television*, May 7, 1970, Committee

Print. Washington: U.S. Government Printing Office, 1970, p. 31.

7   U.S. Congress, Senate, Committee on Foreign Relations, Subcommittee
on Western Hemisphere Affairs, *Guatemala and the Dominican Republic:
A Staff Memorandum*, December 30, 1971. Washington: U.S. Government Printing Office, 1971, pp. 7, 11. U.S. AID officials have, elsewhere, described one of the goals of their programme in Guatemala as
'strengthen(ing) the government's ability to contain the security threat
posed by a serious Communist insurgency movement.' Quoted in Terri
Shaw, 'U.S. Assists Guatemala in "Pacification Programme",' *Washington Post*, April 5, 1971, p. A17.

8   U.S. Congress, House, Subcommittee of the Committee on Appropriations, *Foreign Assistance and Related Agencies Appropriations for
1973, Part 1*, 92nd Congress, 2nd Session. Washington: U.S. Government Printing Office, 1972, p. 749.

9   U.S. Congress, House, Committee on Foreign Affairs, Subcommittee on
National Security Policy and Scientific Development, *Military Assistance Training*, 91st Congress, 2nd Session, October 6, 7, 8, December
8 and 15, 1970. Washington: U.S. Government Printing Office, 1971,
p. 145.

10 U.S. Congress, House, Committee on Foreign Affairs, Subcommittee on
Inter-American Affairs, *Cuba and the Carribbean*, 91st Congress, 2nd
Session, July 8, 9, 10, 13, 20, 27, 31, and August 3, 1970. Washington:
U.S. Government Printing Office, 1970, p. 91–92.

11 *Ibid.*, pp. 98–99.

12 Tad Szulc, 'U.S. Navy's Visa Request Worry Chile,' *New York Times*,
September 5, 1970, p. 3.

13 U.S. Congress, House, Committee on Foreign Affairs, *Foreign Assistance
Act of 1971, Part 2*, 92nd Congress, 1st Session, May 11, 12, 18, 20,
1971. Washington: U.S. Government Printing Office, 1971, pp.
420–421. According to a military attaché of one western country,
' "when the Nixon Government realised that it could not make Popular
Unity see reason, it adopted an attitude which one might objectively
describe as neutral hostility, but this didn't stop Washington keeping
up, and even striving to improve, its relation with the Army.' For this
purpose, the U.S. gave Chile privileged treatment and posted three
military attachés and half a dozen assistants in Santiago. In all, there
were about 30 officers in the whole country who kept in close contact
with the Navy and the Air Force, the Fach.'
Philippe Labreveux, 'Behind the Façade of Unity,' *Manchester Guardian
Weekly* (Le Monde supplement), January 12, 1974, p. 15.

14 Tad Szulc, 'U.S. Gives Chile Credits for Military Purchases,' *New York
Times*, June 30, 1971, pp. 1, 10.

15 U.S. Congress, House, Committee on Foreign Affairs, *Foreign Assistance
Act of 1972, Part 1*, 93rd Congress, 2nd Session, March 14, 15, 20, 21,
22 and 23, 1972. Washington: U.S. Government Printing Office, 1972,
p. 39.

16 Tad Szulc, 'U.S. is Continuing Aid to the Chilean Armed Forces,' *New
York Times*, December 12, 1972, p. 12. Also see U.S. Congress, Senate,
Committee on Foreign Relations, *Foreign Military Sales and Assistance
Act*, 93rd Congress, 1st Session, May 2, 3, 4, and 8, 1973. Washington:
U.S. Government Printing Office, 1973, p. 98.

17 U.S. Congress, House, Subcommittee on Appropriations, *Foreign
Assistance and Related Agencies Appropriations for 1974, Part 1*, 93rd

Congress, 1st Session. Washington: U.S. Government Printing Office, 1973, p. 1198.

18 Testimony of John H. Crimmins, Deputy Assistant Secretary of State for Inter-American Affairs. See U.S. Congress, House, Committee on Foreign Affairs, Subcommittee on Inter-American Affairs, *Aircraft Sales in Latin America*, 91st Congress, 1st Session, April 29 and 30, 1970. Washington: U.S. Government Printing Office, 1970, p. 3.

19 See Presidential Determination No. 73–14, dated May 21, 1973, in *Department of State Bulletin*, July 16, 1973, p. 90. In commenting on this decision to sell fighter aircraft to Argentina, Brazil, Chile, Colombia and Venezuela, Secretary of State Rogers (June 5) emphasised the necessity of lifting legislative restrictions on military sales and grants to Latin America:

'. . . we must also raise the ceiling which current legislation imposes upon military sales and grants. This ceiling is offensive to the Latin Americans who consider it an attempt to control their sovereign right to determine their own defence requirements. The only result of the ceiling has been to encourage the Latin Americans to make their purchases outside the United States.'

U.S. Congress, House, Committee on Foreign Affairs, *Mutual Development Cooperation Act of 1973*, 93rd Congress, 1st Session, May 15, 17, 23, 24, 31; June 5, 6, 11, 12 and 13, 1973. Washington: U.S. Government Printing Office, 1973, p. 257.

20 Quoted in 'Suicide of Dr Allende Reported as Army Attacks Palace and Claims Control of Chile,' *London Times*, September 12, 1973, p. 1.

21 'Chile: The Allende Years, The Coup, Under the Junta—Documents and Analysis,' *IDOC*, No. 58, December 1973, p. 32.

22 Dan Morgan, 'Junta Informed U.S. of Its Plan Before the Coup,' *Washington Post*, September 13, 1973, pp. A1, A12.

23 Dan Morgan, 'Coup Report Discounted, U.S. Claims,' *Washington Post*, September 14, 1973, pp. A1, A13. Senator Kennedy criticised the belated and cryptic official response, pointing out that Allende 'worked within the democratic system to try to effect programmes to carry out (his) philosophy.' Office of Senator Edward M. Kennedy, *Statement on Senate Floor Regarding Events in Chile*, September 13, 1973.

24 *Department of State Bulletin*, October 8, 1973, p. 465.

25 Quoted in Terri Shaw, 'Pre-Coup Activity is Denied by U.S.; *Washington Post*, September 21, 1973, p. A26.

26 Quoted in Tad Szulc, op. cit., p. C5.

27 *Ibid.*

28 *Ibid.*

29 See David Binder, 'Allende Out, Reported Suicide; Marxist Regime in Chile Falls in Armed Forces' Violent Coup: U.S. Not Surprised,' *New York Times*, September 12, 1973, pp. 1, 17.

30 U.S. Congress, Senate, Committee on the Judiciary, Subcommittee to Investigate Problems Connected with Refugees and Escapees, *Refugee and Humanitarian Problems in Chile*, 93rd Congress, 1st Session, September 28, 1973. Washington: U.S. Government Printing Office, 1973, p. 45.

31 Quoted from *Congressional Record*, Senate, February 5, 1974, p. S1237.

32 Quoted in Marvine Howe, '2 Americans Slain in Chile; The Unanswered Questions,' *New York Times*, November 19, 1973, p. 20. An interesting sidelight to the question of U.S.–Chilean military interaction was the following fact: 'Over 100 sailors from Chile were on Guam when the Allende Government was overthrown by the rightist military in September. They were there to take charge of two former U.S. Navy LST amphibious ships. The ships formerly served in Vietnam.' *Friends of Micronesia Newsletter*, Winter, 1974, p. 25.

33 Jeremiah O'Leary, 'United States, Chile Move to Forge New Links,' *Washington Star*, September 25, 1973.

34 'Foreign Banks Come to Chile's Rescue,' *Business Latin America*, December 12, 1973, p. 400; Terri Shaw, 'Chile Gets U.S. Loan For Wheat,' *Washington Post*, October 6, 1973, p. A11.

35 Richard Lawrenre, 'Steps Taken to Resume Aid to Chile,' *Journal of Commerce*, October 17, 1973, p. 1.

36 Quoted in Terri Shaw, op. cit., p. A11.

37 Quoted in Marlisle Simons, 'Chile Flour Shortage is Grave,' *Washington Post*, September 8, 1973, p. A12. Also see Marcel Niedergang, 'Chile's Generals Lower the Curtain,' *Manchester Guardian Weekly* (Le Monde supplement), November 10, 1973, p. 14. U.S. policy makers were aware 'that of all the imports (Chile needs) the food imports are the most critical from a political point of view in the (Allende) Government.' Testimony of John H. Crimmins, Assistant Secretary of State for Inter-American Affairs, before the House Subcommittee on Inter-American Affairs, March 6, 1973. See U.S. Congress, House, *United States-Chilean Relations*, op. cit., p. 24.

38 See Jonathan Kandell, 'Private U.S. Loans in Chile Up Sharply,' *New York Times*, November 12, 1973, pp. 53, 55; 'A Future for Business in Chile,' *Business Week*, September 29, 1973, pp. 30–31; 'Chile: An Uphill Struggle to Revive Business,' *Business Week*, November 17, 1973, p. 41; 'Chile's Offer to Return Firms Meets Favourable Reaction,' *Business Latin America*, November 14, 1973, pp. 363–364. An impasse has presently been reached in the compensation negotiations over Kennecott's demand for $600 million as against the Chilean offer of $300 million. However, Raul Saenz, Economic Adviser to the junta, has stated that the payment would be between $300 million and $600 million. Another condition attached to the generous debt rescheduling involves other major compensation settlements with the U.S. government's Overseas Private Investment Corporation (OPIC). The military junta has already made an initial payment of $1.6 million to OPIC to cover compensation payments made by OPIC to other U.S. investors whose assets were expropriated by the Allende government. See 'Chile: New Debts, Old Debts,' *Latin America Economic Report*, March 15, 1974, p. 42.

39 'Foreign Banks Come to Chile's Rescue,' op. cit., p. 400.

40 Terri Shaw, 'Blockade of Chile Diminishing,' *Washington Post*, October 28, 1973, pp. A1, A17.

41 See Jonathan Kandell, op. cit., pp. 53, 55; 'Foreign Banks Come to Chile's Rescue,' op. cit., p. 400; Everett G. Martin, 'Chile's Rulers Face Huge Economic Woes, Make Some Progress,' *Wall Street Journal*. A number of European countries, Canada, and Brazil also offered lines of credit to the junta.

42 'Foreign Banks Come to Chile's Rescue,' op. cit., p. 400. Cano quoted

in 'Chile Claims Favour of West's Bankers,' *Washington Post*, October 8, 1973, p. A32. In commenting on the possibility of international lines of credit opening up to the junta, Assistant Secretary of State Kubisch stated:

'If the new government adopts sensible programmes that can be supported from abroad, I would expect the World Bank, the Inter-American Development Bank, other government and international agencies, to try and assist if that assistance is warranted.'

See U.S. Congress, Senate, *Refugee and Humanitarian Problems in Chile*, op. cit., p. 36.

43 Richard Lawrence, op. cit., p. 1; 'Foreign Banks Come to Chile's Rescue,' op. cit., p. 400; Embassy of Chile, *Chile: Summary of Recent Events*, February–March 1974, p. 8; *OAS Weekly Newsletter*, March 4, 1974, p. 3.

44 Terri Shaw, 'Chileans, U.S. Agree on Debts,' *Washington Post*, December 22, 1973, p. A3.

45 See George F. W. Telfer, 'Eximbank Weighs Chile Action,' *Journal of Commerce*, January 10, 1974, pp. 1, 3.

46 See Bernard Gwertzman, 'Kissinger Calls on Latins to Join in a "New Dialogue," ' *New York Times*, October 6, 1973, p. 1, 2. The U.S. government has continued to minimise the widespread torture and other repressive policies of the military junta, and has only recently admitted that thousands of people were killed during the coup. See 'Thousands Died During Coup in Chile, Sen. Kennedy Says,' *Washington Post*, February 4, 1974, p. A3. For details on torture, etc. in Chile under the junta, see U.S. Congress, Senate, *Refugee and Humanitarian Problems in Chile*, op. cit.; Extracts from the report of Amnesty International on Human Rights situation in Chile, as read into the *Congressional Record*, Senate, January 24, 1974, pp. S423–S429. During the 1974 foreign assistance appropriations for Chile, there was some Congressional pressure to prevent any of the disbursements from being used for military purposes. A House amendment read that 'and none of these monies shall be used to finance military credit sales to Chile.' It was decisively defeated by a vote of 304 to 102. A Senate amendment stated that 'None of the funds made available under this Act for "Military Assistance," "Security Supporting Assistance," and "Foreign Military Credit Sales," may be used to provide assistance to Chile.' This amendment was agreed to. See *Congressional Record*, House, December 11, 1973, pp. H11121–H11125; *Congressional Record*, Senate, December 17, 1973, pp. S23133–S23135.

CHAPTER IX

Conclusion

As the policies of Chile's military rulers unfold, differences have already appeared among the anti-Allende forces in the United States as well as in Chile. The differences are not insignificant insofar as they reflect not only changes in personnel (civilian *vs.* military), but different positions regarding forms of political rule, the role of the military, and socio-economic policy. What appeared as a united effort between political parties and military officers to prevent the 'communisation of Chile' is no longer visible. The stronger party to the coup, the military, has discarded its political associates, the Frei-led Christian Democrats (PDC), and feels free to impose its own policies through direct representation in the government. In this the military has the support of the smaller upper-class-based National Party and the terrorist ultra-right Fatherland and Liberty Group (together representing about 20 per cent of the electorate).

Through terror, the military was hoping to erase social pressure from the Left; by political exclusion and co-optation, definitely to divide the Christian Democrats; by offering important posts and rewards to the National Party and businessmen, to consolidate an administrative apparatus capable of imposing 'discipline' on labour (with the aid of terror) and securing the cooperation of business; and with an open-door policy to foreign investment, to stimulate foreign loans, credits, and investment to stimulate economic recovery. The 'Brazilian Model' is being projected in Chile over the corpses of 20,000 workers; salaries and wages are being effectively lowered, prices increased, currency devalued, enterprises returned to private owners, and the conditions created for externally induced expansion at the cost of the poor. In the near future, the middle class, business groups, and industrialists will suffer the invasion of large-scale foreign capital which, in the name of efficiency, will eliminate many of those who supported the coup.

Large sectors of the petty bourgeoisie who were in the streets calling for the coup will not be its beneficiaries. As in Brazil, the generals and their economic advisers are looking towards the multi-national corporation and the international banks to re-organise the economy—they, too, have no confidence in the 'entrepreneurial' capacity of the national bourgeoisie, in much the same way they do not trust their bourgeois 'democrats' organised in the PDC to restore and maintain capitalist law and order. If a permanent military-corporate structure is the political instrumentality of the leaders of the coup, large-scale foreign enterprises are their answer to the economic problems facing the country.

The U.S. government long ago gave up the idea that a parliamentary façade is a necessary accompaniment of capitalist development in Latin America. The incapacity of parliamentary régimes to offer guarantees against radicalism and nationalism and their inability to create favourable conditions for foreign investment have for some time provoked U.S. policy-makers and economic influentials into re-thinking the 'best' political formula to serve their interests in Latin America. Brazil provided the test case: while Frei was incapable of preventing a Marxist from winning the presidential elections in Chile, the military dictators in Brazil were attracting loans and investments from all the centres of world capitalism. While U.S. Ambassador Korry was complaining that he had to tell Frei how to put his pants on—figuratively speaking, we assume—the Brazilian military government had practically eliminated all guerrillas, trade unions, strikes, wage demands, thus creating an industrialists' paradise. Whatever promises Frei might have had from Washington before the coup, he had clearly revealed himself as someone the United States could not trust to take over after Allende, despite his espousal of the coup and its terror tactics. After all, it was the military that was willing to bloody its hands, and therefore it was the military which would be willing to take the appropriate measures after the coup to prevent a resurgence of leftism. With the breakdown of the constituted order, and the emergence of a leftist underground, U.S. policy-makers did not believe that Frei would be able to handle the new situation, providing the kind of security to foreign capital that the military could offer, despite the massive and bloody purge. Only a few dissident and peripheral voices of the liberal establishment (*New York Times*, Ford Foundation, *Washington Post*, etc.) felt that the military purge created a secure basis for a return to the parliamentary order and the restoration of Eduardo Frei. The mainstream of U.S. officialdom, the bankers, the international financial agencies, the State Department, the National Security Council, and the multinational corporations have already begun to back the military, its policies and leadership. At best they viewed Frei as a useful but temporary ally on the road to power, suspect for his earlier failure to disregard the democratic verdict of the Chilean people. Now, in the new situation, they are unlikely to offer him more than an honorific secondary post or quiet retirement. The military is not a 'caretaker' government but a permanent political force—the dominant political force in a Chile backed by U.S. economic resources and adapting the Brazilian development strategy to Chilean conditions.

One of the crucial long-term problems facing U.S. policy-makers at the highest level (what can be more accurately described as the historical problems facing the world capitalist system) is the creation of the conditions for economic expansion through private accumulation in dependent capitalist societies. The political formulae or 'frameworks' which are best suited for the capitalist problematic varies with time and place, but each political experience is compared and evaluated in terms of its efficiency in achieving its historic goal. In operational terms the problems of economic expansion and accumulation are essentially political in a double sense : at the level of the state there must exist a dominant political élite willing to subordinate the machinery of government to controlling the working and peasant classes (minimising their political effectiveness, therefore lowering their 'social costs,' i.e. salaries, wages, etc.) and a political orientation which deliberately opens the country to the free flow of capital—especially foreign capital. The existence of the quasi-totalitarian state is especially necessary in those countries which have experienced a high degree of social mobilisation : for there is an inverse relationship between externally induced growth and social mobilisation : the greater the degree of the latter the less likely the former will occur.

Externally induced expansion and accumulation (which appears to be the only source for whatever large-scale industrialisation has taken place within underdeveloped capitalist countries) is dependent upon an authoritarian political framework which can reinforce the requisite social conditions. These social requisites for private accumulation and expansion in dependent capitalist societies include a demobilised working class, non-existent or weak economic nationalist political forces, the elimination or curtailment of wage demands and massive and extensive social welfare programmes and controlled or managed trade unions (falangist-type syndicates). The administrative structure best suited to preserve or enhance these conditions is likely to recruit their top personnel from the propertied groups and 'technocrats' which serve them. The interpenetration of civilian and military bureaucracy is likely especially at the highest and middle levels thus strengthening the power and capacity of the administration to impose its policies on those who benefit least from them. These social requisites and administrative structures are linked through the socio-economic policies of the military-political élite : a deliberate policy of wage and salary reductions of workers is promoted to re-concentrate income in the hands of the foreign and domestic property-classes. Sharp increases in prices and profits are allowed far in excess of the increases in wages; wage workers in fact suffer a relative and absolute decline in real living standards.

The whole process in Chile began with the disaggregation of the state—the creation of a client group among the military. Since seizing power it sought to re-cast the whole state organisation into an administrative instrument for realising the social and political conditions for externally induced expansion. The process of re-integrating Chile within the financial and economic networks of imperialism has proceeded at a fairly rapid rate only because the internal political controls and repression have re-established confidence among the international bankers (though corporate investors appear still to have reservations, especially those investors who would generate *new* capital). The political problem that U.S. policy-makers faced under Allende (of taking political measures to ensure that Chile was reintegrated back into the capitalist world) have been at least temporarily successfully resolved. What remains very doubtful is the medium and long-term durability of a régime whose private sector has in the past shown little inclination to accumulate and invest capital for long-term expansion. And Chile unlike Brazil has neither the large internal market nor passive work force that makes the latter so attractive to the multinationals. In any case Chile may have had its bourgeois counter-revolution too late : if one has Brazil from which to expand throughout the region and beyond, what function can Chile play within the larger imperial design? While Chile may wish to copy 'the Brazilian model', there does not appear to be, from the multinational perspective, any need to duplicate functions. What appears more likely is that Chile will be relegated to the role of raw material and mineral exporter within the larger imperial division of labour. The military's job will be to keep Chile producing within this global pattern.

CHAPTER X

Epilogue

The Chilean military dictatorship has benefited from the new financial largesse shown toward Chile by the international capitalist world: approximately $470 million in loans and credits from the United States, Brazil, Argentina, and the international institutions (see table below); $100 million in short-term credits from a U.S. banking consortium; and scheduled credits of $10 million each from the Banco de Colombia and a Swiss foreign trade financial commission.[1]

Foreign credits granted to Chile since September 1973

		TOTALS
	millions of U.S. $	
GOVERNMENT TO GOVERNMENT LOANS		146.0
From United States	49.0	
Corn purchases	28.0	
Wheat purchases	21.0	
From Brazil	62.0	
Free disposability	50.0	
Sugar purchases	12.0	
From Argentina	35.0	
Reproductive cattle	20.0	
Agricultural machinery	15.0	
INTERNATIONAL INSTITUTIONS		322.8
International Monetary Fund (contingent credit—stand-by)	95.0	
World Bank	18.25	
Pre-investment studies	5.25	
Technical assistance to the public sector	13.0	

Inter-American Development Bank		201.0
Loan announced by IDB's President		
in USA*	30.0	
For agriculture	25.0	
For electrification	70.0	
For irrigation works	45.7	
For reforestation	15.0	
For CORFO projects	10.0	
For social development	6.0	
Andean Development Corporation		8.55
For aircraft leasing	8.55	
TOTAL OF FOREIGN LOANS		468.8

The international banks have made substantial grants to the junta despite the lack of any evidence suggesting an upturn in the economy in the foreseeable future. It is interesting to note in this respect that the $171 million approved by the Inter-American Development Bank was done so on extremely generous terms as far as Chile was concerned—a thirty-year repayment period, with seven years' grace, at two per cent interest per annum.

The U.S. government and U.S. private creditors have also been active in other ways. Chile has received an $11 million military credit from the U.S. government, while 'a group of United States banks, with which Chile has maintained an undischarged debt since 1971, granted a refinancing in the amount of U.S. $124 million shortly after the coup.'[2] Furthermore, the arrangement reached between Chile and her major foreign creditors (U.S., West Germany, Britain, and France) on the rescheduling of Chile's foreign debts 'is expected to release supplier and other types of credit for specific projects . . .'[3]

Despite this influx of capital, industrial production has been steadily declining since October 1973, 'and manufacturers are warning the government that the low purchasing power of consumers may lead to a serious industrial recession.'[4] This situation is a pointed indictment, in particular, of the IMF policies regarding the approval of austerity 'standby' credits ($90 million already granted to Chile since September 1973). It is only during the immediate post-coup period that the junta can argue for a favourable industrial performance—but even that is only in comparison

* No details are given on loan destination.

with the immediate pre-coup period characterised by massive economic sabotage. However, although the industrial production index rose from 110.9 in August and 91.7 in September to 138.0 in October, if we compare December 1973 with December 1972 we find that there was a decline in the index from 132.6 to 125.2[5] Chilean government economists see no signs of a reversal of this present trend.

Economic policies of the imperial centres are largely determined not by abstract criteria of 'creditworthiness' but by the larger politico-economic interests embodied in social régimes which buttress capitalist social relations. Our discussion of U.S. policies toward the Frei, Allende and Pinochet régimes illustrate the inter-relation between the needs of U.S. capitalism and public policy; the bonds between U.S. policy and Chilean propertied groups; the primacy of defending both U.S. and Chilean propertied interests over and against any commitment to parliamentary institutions. The long-term consequences of these international structural bonds and policy commitments suggest that any effort to isolate the purely 'national' (Chilean) or international (U.S.) factor affecting the future development of Chile is a fruitless undertaking. The long-term trend, as indicated by the massive infusion of external financial capital is for the immersion of Chile into a web of economic relations that will in effect shape the contours and thrust of its politico-economic project. Whatever 'national' identity the Chilean ruling class possessed, and whatever its role in 'mediating' external influence in the past, present developments suggest that image is no longer adequate. The 'new Chile' which is emerging from the wreckage of the September 1973 coup increasingly resembles the traditional dependent Latin American country.

NOTES

1 See 'Chile: New Debts, Old Debts,' op. cit., p. 41.
2 *Ibid.*
3 *Ibid.*, p. 42.
4 'Industrial Recession in Chile,' *Latin American Economic Report*, March 15, 1974, p. 43.
5 *Ibid.*